Companions in Grace

A Handbook for Directors of The Spiritual Exercises of St. Ignatius of Loyola

Marian Cowan, C.S.J.
and
John Carroll Futrell, S.J.

Art after 5
"lumps of love"

Sheed & Ward

The Spiritual Exercises of St. Ignatius of Loyola: A Handbook for Directors,
by Marian Cowan, C.S.J. and John Carroll Futrell, S.J., was originally
published by Le Jacq Publishing, Inc. Copyright 1981 by Ministry Training
Services.

Sheed & Ward™ is a service of The National Catholic Reporter Publishing
Company.

Library of Congress Cataloguing-in-Publication Data

Cowan, Marian.
    Companions in grace : a handbook for directors of the spiritual
exercises of St. Ignatius of Loyola / Marian Cowan and John Carroll
Futrell. -- [Rev. ed.]
      p.   cm.
    Includes bibliographical references.
    ISBN 1-55612-667-0 (alk. paper)
    1. Ignatius, of Loyola, Saint, 1491-1556. Exercitia spiritualia.
2. Spiritual exercises. 3. Spiritual direction. I. Futrell, John Carroll.
II. Title.
BX2179.L8C67   1993
248.3--dc20   93-6194
                                                         CIP

Published by: Sheed & Ward
                115 E. Armour Blvd.
                P.O. Box 419492
                Kansas City, MO 64141

To order, call: (800) 333-7373

Table of Contents

Preface to the Revised Edition

THIS HANDBOOK FOR DIRECTORS OF THE SPIRITUAL EXERCISES was originally written in response to an expressed need for a tool to assist new directors in their companioning of others through a very graced time in their lives. Since it was first published in 1981 under the title *The Spiritual Exercises of St. Ignatius of Loyola: A Handbook for Directors*, the book has proved extremely helpful to any number of directors, those just beginning as well as those more seasoned and well acquainted with the Ignatian Exercises. And still the need continues to grow.

In recent years we are witnesses to a burgeoning interest in the *Spiritual Exercises* of St. Ignatius. More and more people from many walks of life are turning to the Exercises as a school of prayer and a mode of deepening their relationship with God. This growing desire for a protracted, individually guided experience of spiritual deepening has brought a concomitant growth in programs to train competent directors of the Exercises. This, in turn, has prompted the publication of a new, revised edition of the handbook.

As co-authors of the handbook, we chose to maintain the style unique to each of us by writing various sections as individuals rather than writing each section together in an emergent new style. All the sections dealing with the dynamics of the Exercises, the commentaries on Ignatius' Rules, the reference material and the appendices were written by John Futrell. Marian Cowan wrote all the sections dealing with movement into each step and ways of proceeding throughout the Exercises.

Throughout the book, *Spiritual Exercises* (italicized) refers chiefly to Ignatius' book; otherwise, Spiritual Exercises refers to the activities within a retreat.

As mentioned in the Preface to the First Edition, it is presumed that the reader has at hand a copy of the *Spiritual Exercises* for ready reference. Reference numbers within this handbook, often in square brackets, refer to the paragraph numbers accompanying the text of the *Spiritual Exercises* common in all editions since 1928.

The major revision has been to honor contemporary theology, which states clearly that God is neither male nor female but both. Thus we have changed all references to God into inclusive language. The rest of the revisions have been minor corrections, so that the wealth of material in the body of the text remains.

It is our hope that this handbook will continue to be a source of help and inspiration to all those persons who accompany others in the Spiritual Exercises of St. Ignatius. We applaud Sheed & Ward for their vision and conviction that this will be so. Together we present this revised edition of the handbook "for the greater glory of God."

Marian Cowan, C.S.J.
John Carroll Futrell, S.J.
Feast of St. Ignatius, 1993

Preface to the First Edition

DURING RECENT YEARS, MORE AND MORE PEOPLE, LAY, RELI-gious, and priests—have been expressing the desire to make directed retreats according to the method of the *Spiritual Exercises* of St. Ignatius of Loyola. Thus, the need has been recognized to train such persons as well-qualified directors of the Spiritual Exercises. Even experienced directors speak of the need for continuing reflection and dialogue with other directors in order to grow constantly in their mastery of the art of direction. To meet these needs various centers are engaged in training retreat directors, and a growing list of written aids is being published. At this time, it seems that a useful service is to provide a practical handbook for directors, which may also be helpful to persons preparing to make a thirty-day directed retreat. Therefore, the goal of this book is to try to perform this service.

In this handbook, the term "directed retreat" is used to refer to "one-on-one" daily direction of an individual retreatant by an individual director. This is clearly a different dynamic from that of a preached retreat, or even that of a "semidirected" or "guided" retreat, which includes one or more daily talks to a whole group of retreatants and, usually, less than a daily conference by the director with an individual retreatant. A directed retreat might continue for an entire month or longer, or for a shorter period. It might be given over a period of months to a person continuing the ordinary routine of duties, usually designated as the "Nineteenth Annotation" or "Daily Life Retreat" (see Appendix 4). It might also be several days of "directed prayer." The retreat might involve going through the entire *Spiritual Exercises* as presented in St. Ignatius' little book, or it might involve going through only part of them. All of these are ways of directing and making the Exercises.

Because the paradigm for making the Spiritual Exercises is the thirty-day retreat outlined in the book by St. Ignatius, this handbook will treat specifically that form. Since other retreats are given within the dynamic of that form, the handbook can also be a useful aid to directors of these (see Appendices 5 and 6).

Since this is a handbook, it is assumed that the reader will have the text of the *Spiritual Exercises* available and will constantly refer to it. The sources from which we, the co-authors, have drawn the contents of the book are historical and theological studies of the *Spiritual Exercises,* as well as years of experience in directing the Exercises for thirty days and for shorter or longer periods. Through this experience we have come to believe that it can be particularly helpful to our readers to have the reflections of two directors as an indication of the varieties of approach possible when directing the Spiritual Exercises.

We first present a reflection on the general dynamics of directing and making the Exercises. Following that description of the growth movement of the thirty-day Spiritual Exercises, we offer reflections on the dynamics of the successive stages of growth and then indications both of practical ways for directing the retreatant through these various stages and of the specific exercises within each stage. Included in the practical sections are various considerations regarding the social dimension of peace and justice; although the retreatant is engaged in a highly personal experience during the Exercises, the accent is certainly apostolic. In the third part of the book, those rules by Ignatius important for the retreat's dynamic are considered. Finally, a series of appendices provide further practical aids for direction of the Spiritual Exercises.

In one sense, this has been a very difficult book to write. During the years in which we have been directing people through the *Spiritual Exercises,* we have found ourselves growing in an understanding of the Exercises and, therefore, developing in the way we present them. We have not completed that growth and development; it is our hope never to consider it finished. No two people approach prayer in exactly the same way. Each retreatant is unique and individual in his or her spiritual journey; therefore, the Exercises must be adapted to the person going through them. Thus the difficulty: will the reader interpret this statement of *a* way to apply the Exercises or as *the* way one should go about it? It is not *the* way. There is not one single way that is correct, with all others faulty. The practical directions given here are simply an attempt to help directors of the Spiritual Exercises to find the proper way for them at a given time for a given retreatant. We therefore urge the reader to let the words in this book simply be what they are intended to be: an assist.

Probably the most important practical help to John Carroll Futrell, S.J., in his own direction of the Spiritual Exercises, has been the tutelage of Jean Laplace, S.J., provided through two sets of privately distributed mimeographed notes, one a commentary on the thirty-day Spiritual Exercises, the other notes on directing the Exercises during ten days.[1]

Drawing heavily and at times directly from these notes, Father Futrell is deeply grateful for the kind permission of Father Laplace to use his material. Marian Cowan, C.S.J., in her reflections on the social dimension of the Exercises, has been strongly influenced by the work of Michael J. O'Sullivan, S.J., in his unpublished Master's thesis entitled "Towards a Social Hermeneutic of the Spiritual Exercises with an Application to

---

1. Father Laplace has published as a book a condensation of notes on directing the Spiritual Exercises during ten days: *Une Experience de la vie dans l'Esprit* (Paris: Chalet, 1972). There is an English translation, *An Experience of Life in the Spirit* (Chicago: Franciscan Herald Press, 1977).

the Annotations." In keeping with a handbook, the co-authors have deliberately kept references to a minimum.

It is our pleasant duty to express our gratitude to many experienced directors who have helped us to grow in our appreciation of the Spiritual Exercises, to retreatants who have blessed us by seeking our direction, to directors with whom we have been on teams, and to the 1977 retreat team at Institut Roncalli, in Salatiga, Indonesia, who urged us to write down these reflections.

Special thanks are due to Mary Louise Begert, D.M.J., James M. Burke, S.J., Margaret Carroll, P.B.V.M., David L. Fleming, S.J., Ferdinand Hamma, S.J., Michael Harter, S.J., Eugene Merz, S.J., and Thomas Prag, S.J., for reading and commenting on this handbook and, especially to Janice Futrell, O.S.B., for editing the text and to Donna Paladino and Carmelita Becker for careful typing.

Marian Cowan, C.S.J.
John Carroll Futrell, S.J.
Feast of Saint Ignatius 1980

PART I

Dynamics of Directing and Making the Spiritual Exercises of St. Ignatius of Loyola

CHAPTER 1

Introduction to the Exercises

MY APPROACH IN THIS REFLECTION WILL BE PRACTICAL. THUS, after giving some necessary background on the dynamic movement of the Spiritual Exercises, I shall offer some practical general considerations on directing them and on being directed in making them.

A person directing the Spiritual Exercises approaches the *one* Christian spirituality—the movement of all things to the Godhead through Jesus Christ in the Holy Spirit—through the way of a particular school of spirituality, that of the Ignatian *Spiritual Exercises*. Fundamentally, there is only one Christian spirituality, one movement through Jesus Christ to the Godhead: the *sequela C.....sti,* the following of Christ, presented to us in the Gospel.

Nevertheless, during the history of the Church there have developed describably different ways of facilitating this movement, according to the variety of personalities and of temperaments and of charisms of the great Christian spiritual masters, one of whom is St. Ignatius of Loyola. It is important to note, however, that the Ignatian way is not a "Jesuit" thing. Ignatius himself experienced, wrote, and directed the *Spiritual Exercises* as a layman during many years before he discerned that he was called to found a religious order. Many religious congregations and individuals follow the spirituality of the Ignatian *Spiritual Exercises* without being Jesuits. Many non-Jesuits are first-rate directors of the Exercises.

A twofold objective marks the way of the Spiritual Exercises: (1) the Word of God revealed through Jesus Christ; (2) the specific Ignatian approach in the historical spirituality contained in the *Spiritual Exercises*.

Thus, not just anything can be called the Spiritual Exercises of St. Ignatius. The Ignatian way is not the only excellent way to enter into the movement. However, it is a concrete and documentable way that is specifically different from other ways. For example, Ignatian contemplation is a particular method of prayer among a great variety of Christian methods of prayer, each differentiated by its own specific directions.

A problem for some persons during recent years has been a feeling of antipathy to the historical vocabulary and acculturated images of the Ignatian *Spiritual Exercises*, or a turning off of procedures previously learned in a formalistic way. To solve this problem, it is necessary to return to Ignatius and the *Spiritual Exercises* revealed by accurate historical documentation. Ignatius was never formalistic or *a priori*. In the *Spiritual Exercises* he simply describes, using the only language he had in his era, the way of going to the Godhead through Jesus Christ and the procedures that he himself had experienced as a powerful means of growing in the Lord. If radical changes of historical cultures and misunderstanding of the intentions of Ignatius have caused formalistic teaching of the Exercises, it becomes necessary to recover the reality of this way, even to "redeem" terminology and procedures.

It seems important to me to help people make a real effort, even repeated efforts, to enter into the objective dynamic of the Spiritual Exercises in order to discover by experience whether what at first turned them off will in fact ultimately be very helpful. During recent years, it has been necessary to do this with many objective elements of Christian spirituality, and I have found that by redeeming terminology and procedures, it has been possible to assist people through experience to a rediscovery of authentic values—for example, daily examination of consciousness, spiritual direction, silent retreats, and even just praying.

Whether one uses the historical vocabulary of the book of the *Spiritual Exercises* or not, the fundamental reality of the Exercises is movement through an experiential process, not a verbal text;[1] it would be possible to adhere slavishly to the verbal text without accurately leading the retreatant through this movement. Identifiable stages of growth within the spiritual journey are mapped out in the *Spiritual Exercises*, along with identifiable means of reaching the progressive stages within the total movement. A key function of the director is to help the retreatant to stay within this movement, to move from and build upon each progressive stage of growth, and to reach successive goals that lead to the culmination of the movement. This fact highlights the centrality of the *id quod volo*; the specific grace to be prayed for in the various exercises. The *id quod volo*—where the exercitant is to rest in prayer—functions as a prevailing guide for all the behaviors and the changes of environment that facilitate the ongoing movement.

Thus, the objective element provides the control of the subjective element in directing and making the Exercises. The retreatant is always confronted by the Word of God as it unfolds in Scripture and in the life of Jesus. The "movements" that the retreatant experiences, therefore, respond to what is proclaimed as that word touches this unique person in life with God now. Accordingly, the personal means helpful for one's coming to more and more open response to God are always fitted to the demands of the revealed word:

God presenting Godself . . .
Resting in the Heart of Christ . . .

---

1.   Cf. David L. Fleming, S.J., *The Spiritual Exercises of St. Ignatius, A Literal Translation and a Contemporary Reading* (St. Louis: The Institute of Jesuit Sources, 1978). See especially pp. xv-xvii. His entire "Contemporary Reading" is exemplification of what he states there.

> through him to the Godhead . . .
> in this mystery for God's People.

For example, during the Third Week of the Exercises, everything is geared to help the retreatant to come to a profound affective identification with Jesus on the cross, to a deep realization of his love for all humanity, and to a passionate desire to be with him in his way of saving all.

Persons whose approach to the one Christian spirituality is specifically that of the Ignatian Spiritual Exercises have a spiritual framework within which they operate as retreat directors. Their use of Scripture texts and of the key meditations of the Spiritual Exercises results from this fact and reflects it.[2] For example, I experience myself as always giving direction within the dynamic movement of the Exercises, even if what a particular retreatant needs now is eight days of deepening one spiritual attitude—what has been called eight days of "directed prayer."

As has been noted, successive stages of growth in the movement toward the Godhead through Jesus Christ in the Holy Spirit have been evidenced both in the spiritual doctrine given in sacred Scripture and in the funded experience of people living Christian spirituality for hundreds of years. Different schools of spirituality, including the Ignatian Spiritual Exercises, have various ways of helping people to grow through these stages. The *Exercises* presents them as follows:

1. *First Principle and Foundation* [23]. The goal is to realize deeply the faith vision of all reality as the dynamic movement of God's creative love toward the fulfillment of God's

---

2.   These key meditations have often been identified as: First Principle and Foundation [23]; the Kingdom of Christ [91-99]; A Meditation on Two Standards [136-148]; Three Classes of Men [149-157]; Three Kinds of Humility [165-168]; and Contemplation to Attain Love of God [230-237]. Reference numbers within the text refer to the paragraph numbers accompanying the text of the *Spiritual Exercises* common in all editions since 1928, including the critical text presented in *Exercitia Spiritualia: Textus* (Rome: Historical Institute of the Society of Jesus, 1969).

eternal purpose (Eph. 1-10).[3] Through this realization, I am graced with a profound sense of the reality and majesty of God and of God's personal love for me in creating me. I recognize God's personal call to me to open myself and to be filled with God's love and life, and I perceive God's unending fidelity to me. Consequently, I seek total spiritual freedom—expressed by Ignatius in the words "make ourselves indifferent"—in order to surrender all my desires to God's concrete call to me, known or yet to be discovered, so that in all ways I shall always "praise, reverence, and serve God our Lord." Thus, all of my desires and choices and uses of creatures will become ordered to my own profound ruling desire—to move more and more to God as I discover God's every new call to me, "in order that the glory of his gracious gift, so graciously bestowed on us in his Beloved, might redound to his praise" (Eph. 1:6). This faith vision, then, will focus the movement of my entire being toward God, which will lead to discernment of all God's daily calls to me in light of the election of my life vocation. I shall always see and choose and do, no matter what the cost, what God calls me to do.

2. *First Week* [24-90]. The goal is to be graced with intense sorrow and tears for my sins, while realizing that God loves me nevertheless—just as I am—and forgives me everything through the death on the cross of God's Son, Jesus Christ. Thus, I realize my own radical incapacity to follow God's call to me, except in and through Jesus Christ. Defenseless, I stand open before the gratuity of God's love.

3. *The Kingdom of Christ* [91-99]. The goal is to realize that, in spite of everything, I am called by Jesus Christ to labor with him in accomplishing his mission to save all human beings, through his way of poverty and humiliations and

---

3. See "Dynamics of the First Principle and Foundation" in Part II.

such

suffering. I experience as God's personal call to me, through Jesus Christ in and through the Church, the call of the Holy Spirit deep within me.

4. *Second Week* [101-189]. The goal is the transformation of my deep operational attitudes into those of Jesus through contemplation of his life, so that I will follow him unconditionally in the particular way to which he calls me (Choice of a Way of Life [169-188]; Reformation of One's Way of Living in One's State of Life [189]). These attitudes of Jesus are shown forth in the mysteries of his human life, continually and repeatedly contemplated, and they are focused by Ignatius in three key meditations.

   A. *A Meditation on Two Standards* [136-148]. The goal is to realize that laboring with Christ to bring the Kingdom to be demands direct confrontation with the active forces of evil in myself and in the world. Essential is the ability to discern how I am being moved away from this labor and how I am being moved toward it— namely, the following of Christ in his way of poverty, humiliations, and humility.

   B. *Three Classes of Persons* [149-157]. The goal is to be graced with choosing decisively and constantly to follow Jesus Christ in his way of bringing the Kingdom to be as he now calls me, no matter what the cost.

   C. *Three Kinds of Humility* [165-168]. The goal is to experience such passionate, personal love for Jesus that I simply want *to be with him* wherever he goes—literally poor and humiliated—so that I can labor with him to bring the Kingdom to be his way. "So Christ was treated before me " [167].

5. *Third Week* [190-209]. The goal is to deepen personal love and compassion for the suffering Jesus, so that I desire to go all the way to Calvary with him; because he went there

first out of love for all humanity, I realize I can thus labor with him for the Kingdom.

6. *Fourth Week* [218-229]. The goal is through contemplation of the Risen Jesus to become able always to see his victory *in* the cross. Because in rising from the dead he gave the guarantee of the final success of God's saving plan, I desire the gifted strength to follow him in his Church all the way to the cross in the joy of the Resurrection.

7. *Contemplation to Attain Love of God* [230-237]. The goal of this entire movement of spiritual growth is to be able to live ongoing discernment of God's call to me in every event of daily life and, so, to find God in all things. Ignatius focuses this final goal in the Contemplation to Attain Love of God, where I pray for the grace to see that *all* things are a vehicle for mutual communication with God. Thus seeing God in and through all, I shall love God in all things and all things in God.

As is well known, the book of the *Spiritual Exercises* emphasizes this spiritual movement as being toward the "election" [169-188], which is the authentic discernment of the call of God to a person to respond for a lifetime through a specific Christian vocation. Clearly, the typical regular retreat of most persons will be concerned, rather, with deepening the movement toward God within a vocation already discerned and responded to or, at times, with handling crucial choice points within this movement [189]. When the purpose of the Exercises is not an actual life choice but personal spiritual renewal, the retreatant should be oriented toward a more profound awareness of the spiritual motives directing and organizing one's own life. Above all, this means to disengage from among the multiplicity of elements that compose the complex reality of this individual's spiritual life, its integrating core, actually to arrive at the heart of this person's life.

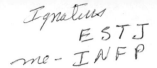

To summarize this background on the dynamic movement of the Spiritual Exercises, the goal is to assist a person's growth into total spiritual freedom, with the unique ruling desire being to choose God, all ways always. Then, a person can live a discerning life—finding God in all things and responding to God's actual word here and now in every concrete situation through all of one's choices and actions. The subjective element of the discernment process is provided by Ignatius' Rules for the Discernment of Spirits [313-336] while the objective element is provided by his Rules for Thinking with the Church [352-370].[4] Once again, the objective element always controls the subjective element. The director must help the retreatant to grow in the ability to live always this ecclesial spiritual discernment.

Some practical general considerations on directing the Spiritual Exercises and on being directed in them comprise the remainder of this chapter.

An environment to facilitate the movement toward God is offered by Ignatius in the Additional Directions [73-86], the hours of prayer, and the ongoing dynamic of the *id quod volo*. Helped by the director to live within this special environment chosen for thirty days, the retreatant can better clarify his or her awareness of the positive and negative forces at work within self. The Exercises call a person to identify these many forces operating simultaneously at multiple levels, all in relation to God's gratuity. Enabled to recognize these forces through the Rules for the Discernment of Spirits [313-336], the person can go out after the retreat, empowered to act upon one's real life environment through a decisive free choice of God—election. In our contemporary world, for example, each person by acculturation is caught up in sinful structures that institutionalize injustice into a network of systems of exploitation and oppression of whole groups of peoples in the "global village." Unconsciously

---

4.   See Part III.

conditioned into consumerism, racism, and the many other attitudes that limit interior freedom and foster a multitude of inordinate desires, a person often gives at least passive cooperation with these systemic injustices. Thus, it is vital that the retreatant bring these particular "unfreedoms" to conscious awareness. Otherwise, it will be impossible to identify the movements that arise out of this acculturation within one's life environment and to be open to the opposing movements of the Holy Spirit calling one to resist these and actively to struggle for social justice. As the contemporary Church has repeatedly pointed out, living the Gospel today constitutively includes the promotion of social justice.[5]

Being certain that a person is truly prepared to make a thirty-day retreat is very important, especially today with the widespread desire, even a faddishness, about making one. The director should make certain that the prospective retreatant is in adequate psychological and physical health to undertake the Spiritual Exercises. Furthermore, it is most desirable that the person will already have made at least one eight-day directed retreat. Finally, it will be futile to begin the retreat if the person does not have the right dispositions. These dispositions are described by Ignatius in the Introductory Observations [1-20].

1. One must be truly disposed to exercise self, that is, to make the personal effort required to do the Exercises [1].

2. One must be truly disposed, at least in sincere desire, to open self unconditionally to God's gift of Self through the Exercises [5].

3. One must be ready to spend the hour of the prayer period, at times even more, in a true effort to pray, even when in desolation [12-13].

Father Laplace comments that to spend a full hour, even a little more in order not to judge prayer by the superficial

---

5. See note 5 in "Dynamics of the First Week," in Part II.

impressions it causes, is the only way to root oneself in faith, going beyond the level of feelings and even of understanding. Simply to have remained one hour before God in faith is an excellent exercise. Indeed, the four or five hours of prayer are the great power of the Exercises—their secret. The retreatant must persevere in prayer until he or she knows that the prayer is answered in God's own way.

4. The retreatant must be truly disposed to be totally open to the director, reporting all the movements experienced [17].

5. The retreatant must be truly desirous of making as much progress as possible, disposed to leave not only the ordinary life environment but also all preoccupation with it, simply opening self completely to the movements of the Holy Spirit during the Exercises. It is necessary to relax, to forget all else, and, like Abraham (Gen. 12:1-3), to leave all in an exodus that enables one to enter into the retreat to seek only God [20].

Father Laplace observes that the beginning takes time. To let oneself go: this is the hardest thing to do. This should be the only effort: to let oneself go into the silence. Thus, the truth can reveal itself slowly, gradually, in the peaceful and silent rhythm of the Spiritual Exercises. As "good soil" (Matt. 13), which receives the word of God in faith, the retreatant seeks the reality under the words just as one seeks the reality under the appearances in the Eucharist. One advances in the measure that he or she lets go of all preconceived ideas, in order to be nothing but a listener—open to the light that God will give. The condition for such interior listening is a purification of one's own manner of praying and listening. The retreatant must enter into the silence of the heart, turning off any little interior film of fantasizing, of criticizing, or of seeking beautiful ideas or superficial feelings.

Thus, in order to enter into the retreat with its First Principle and Foundation [23] the person must have these dispositions and be ready to work at the exercises—to try, but failing, to begin again; to accept the groping by putting self under the action of God and remaining calm; to make an effort without tension, within grace, not a nervous effort, but one in which God is present. The initial effort needed to enter into a deep and beautiful silence gives way little by little to something tremendous and profound in which one eventually feels at ease. The retreatant must make the effort to create a solitude, a "desert." So there must be nothing harsh or mechanical. One must be very flexible in order to find one's own rhythm.

The insistence of Ignatius that a retreatant must be led forward in the movement of the Exercises according to one's own dispositions and capacity as well as the graces received is made very clear in Introductory Observation [18]. This illustrates, once again, that a director is giving the Spiritual Exercises by introducing a person into their dynamic movement, whether or not it is possible to complete the movement of the entire four weeks. The use of Scripture texts is always in function of that movement in the particular retreatant, with the key meditations focused on special, crucial moments of growth within the movement. Consequently, indications of texts and of meditations for prayer are determined by the director according to the individual's place within the stages of growth of the one Christian spirituality. The first thing necessary for the director, then, is to find out where this person is, perhaps actually pre-First Week.[6]

Practically, if a person clearly is in pre-First Week, I give texts for prayer focused on the reality and majesty of God and of God's personal love, moving gradually to texts to help the individual to receive the specific grace of the Principle and Foundation [23]: total openness to whatever might be God's call

---

6. See Appendix 1 in Part IV.

to this person, with the unique ruling desire only to enter more and more into union with God.[7] When and if it is clear that this grace is operative within a person, I spend only a short time to renew the realization of it before entering into the exercises of the First Week. The control by which the director determines when to take the retreatant into a new stage of the movement—for example, First Week, Second Week, etc.—is the recognition that the retreatant indeed has reached the goal, that is, has received the grace of the previous stage, upon which and out of which the movement of the new stage proceeds.

What, then, does the director do during a direction session? He or she gives spiritual direction.[8] Above all, being a loving, listening presence is the norm of all that the director does. The Desert Fathers, at the beginning of the tradition of spiritual direction in Christian spirituality, identified three causes of the efficacy of spiritual direction: (1) the faith of the directee, who trusts that God truly will work through this director to help the person grow toward God; (2) the director's constant prayer for the directee, bringing the grace of God to be the most powerful element in the direction itself; (3) the spiritual quality of the mutual conversation of the director and the directee, through which the Holy Spirit works the spiritual good of both.

Counting upon these three causes for the success of the retreat, the person directing the Spiritual Exercises must be able to make her/himself truly present to the other, as one who attentively listens with love. Above all, the director is never judgmental, never shocked at what is heard. One does not give homilies or teach or develop one's own insights. The director does offer:

1. *Questions* to help the retreatant to clarify his or her own experience of God and to do his or her own discernment, in order to recognize and to respond to the call of God;

---

7. See Appendix 1 for a listing of such tests in Part IV.

8. See Appendix 2 in Part IV.

2. *Models* drawn from the director's own experience or from his or her knowledge of the funded experience of the Church or from the experience of directing other persons, which are given as hypotheses that may or may not illuminate what the retreatant is now experiencing;

3. *Information,* but only when the retreatant is experiencing a spiritual problem, which is actually the result of lack of information or of misinformation. The director may also be called upon to help a particular retreatant to clarify images of God operative in one's prayer, or to lead the person through a pedagogy of prayer to help the retreatant to practice the various methods of prayer of the Exercises.

During a retreat, the director presents the directives for the day, briefly explaining the spirit of these and the particular grace to be prayed for (*id quod volo!*), in function of where and how God is leading this retreatant. The director also indicates Scripture texts for prayer, divided for the periods of prayer.[9] One may give a few words on the pertinent dynamics of the Spiritual Exercises and offer suggestions in accord with the Additional Observations [73-90] for shaping the environment to facilitate the particular stage within the movement toward God in which the retreatant is presently engaged.

And what does the retreatant talk about during the direction session? This person should report what he or she has experienced during and outside of the prayer periods.

1. Was I faithful to the prayer or wasn't I? Did I spend the time, and why or why not? Did I find the place and environment and my physical positions helpful for my prayer?

2. How about my fidelity to and experience of the retreat silence, which is central to the dynamic of the Exercises and

---

9.   See Appendix 3 in Part IV.

which should deepen constantly during the retreat, moving toward all-pervasive union with God?

3. What is the quality of my silence? Am I finding it boring, restless, bringing me to dwell on the past; or is it becoming more and more a calm, deep silence of the heart?

4. Do I enter into profound silence in beginning my prayer periods, in order to "get myself together" and to be really present to the Lord?

5. How do I use my time outside the prayer periods? Do I run to reading, or am I more and more reflecting upon what God has shown me, more and more moving toward God, from getting up in the morning to going to bed at night?

6. Am I writing a great deal or not at all? It is good for many people to write down their reflections, lights, emerging patterns of God's action, and so on. But there can be a temptation in some people to start writing a book, which is not what a retreat is about!

Thus, the essential content of what the retreatant shares with the director during the direction session is what has been going on in his or her prayer and throughout the day—what has been experienced: joys, fears, consolation, desolation, strengthening of faith, hope, love; emptiness, aridity, distractions, attractions, calls apparently from God, gifted freedom, lack of freedom, peace, turmoil, presence or absence of God, and so on. The retreatant should note and share any new lights and insights into the ongoing action of the Holy Spirit being experienced. The director should be told about difficulties that have come up and persisted, about what is perceived as impeding progress, about what God is communicating, and about temptations which, often during a retreat, are felt more than usual, especially in movements counter to trust in God or, sometimes, with respect to faith.[10]

What attitudes should be operative within the director? Above all, one must have great trust that the Spirit of God, who worked through Balaam's ass (Num. 22:21-33), is working through me, so that I direct with great peace and total confidence in God's love for and guidance of the retreatant. In this great drama of spiritual growth, the true director is God, the chief actor is the exercitant, while the human director has the chief supporting role. However, the director must also trust self, trust his or her own experience, in judging where this retreatant is within the movement of the Spiritual Exercises and how to proceed from there.

For example, Ignatius is most insistent that the director not allow the retreatant to move on to the Second Week of the Exercises until he or she clearly has attained the fruit of the First Week, which has been well articulated as "to stand without defenses before the gratuity of God's love." How can the director be certain that the retreatant truly has come to this? I can know this in the way I know anything at all about the mystery of another human being: through the experience of all the many levels of human mutual communication. I know that certain people love me for instance; I would stake my life on this. Also, I, as a priest, make the judgment that people are properly disposed to receive absolution in the sacrament of reconciliation. I do this in peace, with moral certitude and with trust in God. In the same way, when giving direction, I make a judgment in function of all

---

10. In the Introductory Observations [1-20], Ignatius makes it clear that the retreatant should be totally open with the director about one's own fidelity to the directives for making the Exercises, and about one's observance of the Additional Directions [73901, as well as about the movements and insights experienced [3]; [6]; [11]; [12]; [13]; [17]; [20]. Father Edward Pereyra, S.J., in a Directory written in 1562, listed the matters given in my text for sharing with the director during the First Week and the Second Week. *Directoria Exercitiorum Spiritualium,* 1540-1599 (C Rome: Historical Institute of the Society of Jesus, 1955) pp. 152-153, 161.

the human communication received from the retreatant, and I move forward in peace with trust in God.

Another key attitude of the good director is patience—giving time for the Holy Spirit to work in the retreatant, waiting for the moment when the retreatant can bear it before confronting; but, indeed, confronting the person when this is necessary to help him or her to grow spiritually.

Finally, it is important that the director be discerning the movements that go on within self while directing another person, to make sure that I do not give way to the temptation to manipulation, or to seek myself, but that I remain simply an instrument of the Lord.

Various directors find various methods helpful for following the movements of the spirit in each retreatant. Some directors write down their impressions after each direction session. Personally, I take notes during the direction session; and I give these notes to each retreatant at the end of the retreat.

Many persons find that, when it is possible, directing a retreat with a team of directors is very helpful. Daily team meetings provide not only a support system on the human level of friendship and relaxation, but also on the level of shared prayer for one another and for all the retreatants. Furthermore, the team sharing provides invaluable mutual help for giving good direction, as each director can consult with all the others about procedures of direction. The problem of confidentiality is solved by a method of guarding anonymity of the retreatants, accomplished best by seeing to it that no director knows the identities of the persons being directed by the others.

Some teams of directors also avoid personal pronouns, which would indicate whether a directee is a man or a woman.

The Spiritual Exercises, then, are one way to enter into the movement of the one Christian spirituality toward the Father through Jesus Christ in the Holy Spirit. Making a thirty-day directed retreat according to the way of the Exercises can be for many people today a leap ahead in holiness, in being filled with

God, in order to share God with all the people whose lives touch ours.

A Prayer When Beginning to Make a Retreat

Gracious God,
> give me intimate understanding and a relish of
> > the truth.
> Help me to enter with total generosity toward you.
> I offer you my entire will and liberty
> > that your Divine Majesty may dispose of me and
> > all I possess
> > > according to your most holy will.
> Teach me to make an effort without tension, within
> > grace,
> > where you are present—
> > > into a deep and beautiful silence.
> I ask you to communicate yourself to me and to
> > inflame me
> > with your love and praise
> and to dispose me for the way in which I can better
> > serve you in the future.

PART II

Dynamics of the Stages of the Spiritual Exercises and Indications for Directors of Ways of Proceeding

CHAPTER 2

Preparing for the Exercises

The Preparation Time: A Way of Proceeding

The way a retreatant is introduced into the actual experience of the Spiritual Exercises sets the tone for the entire journey. It is up to the director to lead the retreatant to a relaxed, receptive stance before the Lord. The preliminary conference, therefore, is important.

If the retreat begins with an evening celebration of the Eucharist, the liturgy can well draw the retreatant into the reverence and calm that characterize openness before God. Sometime the same evening it is good for the director to meet with the retreatant to clarify expectations, to allay fears, and to establish the time of the conferences. If five or six persons are making the Spiritual Exercises during the same thirty days in an individually directed way, the director can handle the preliminaries by meeting, for this one time, with the group.

Some things to be addressed at this time are: (1) relaxing into the retreat; (2) knowing that God, who loves the retreatant beyond all measure, is the one with whom the next thirty days will be spent; (3) dropping specific expectations; (4) realizing that making a retreat like this is not selfish, but rather very apostolic in thrust; (5) going over the Introductory Observations that pertain to the retreatant—[1]; [3]; [4]; [5]; [11]; [12]; [13]; [16]; [17]; [20].

Although this preliminary conference can be very short, it should not end without directions for prayer to be done before the first assigned conference. One very fine way of moving into a knowledge of where the retreatant is vis-a-vis God, and thus to find the take-off point from which to build the retreat, is to ask the retreatant to spend some time getting in touch with those passages of Scripture that have been speaking to him or her lately, which seem to haunt, or which have become favorites. The retreatant should be able to speak about these passages the next day, not as an exegesis, but in an experiential way; for example, "What this says to me is . . ."

The first days of the retreat are often best left unstructured. Rather than fitting oneself into a structure of established periods for prayer, the retreatant might better be advised to let the day flow—to have formal prayer as one is moved to it, discovering the length of a prayer period that is most comfortable at this time; to spend the day "with God," becoming conscious of God's presence particularly in the movement from one activity to another, such as walking or going to lunch. It is not too early for the retreatant to begin the reflection time following each prayer period and noting the various movements that occurred in prayer, nor is it too early to introduce an examen of how the day progressed. Both of these reflection times can be refined later according to numbers 77 and 90 in the Spiritual Exercises.

The first few days can also be profitably spent in a sort of "tuning up of the senses." This presents a real way of moving into the First Principle and Foundation without addressing the text directly. "Tuning the senses" simply means standing receptive to the gifts of the Lord, using all five senses. Concentrating on one sense at a time, the retreatant receives creation, for example, through the eyes, seeing as far as one possibly can, then beholding things up close, such as color, texture, light and shade; then through the ears, noticing how one tunes in some sounds at the expense of others; then taste, savoring the food at meals instead of eating dutifully; and so on through the other senses. There are two major reasons for this: (1) for the retreatant to grow in a stance of radical receptivity before the Lord, and (2) for the tuning up of the interior senses that accompanies the exercising of the exterior senses. Resulting graces are often a letting-go of inhibitions, an increase of vulnerability, and an awareness of being gifted.

Readiness

The awareness that "all is gift," and more especially that "all is gift FOR ME," is an indication of readiness for the full presentation of the First Principle and Foundation [23].

Dynamics of the First Principle and Foundation [23]

With the consideration entitled First Principle and Foundation, Ignatius grounds the entire dynamic movement of the Spiritual Exercises in the faith view of all reality, the faith view of the biblical people of God. This consideration, then, is the initiation of the retreatant into the ongoing process of exercises opening one to graces that will order his or her whole life to God.

Biblical faith provides the vision of all reality—of the whole physical universe and the whole of humanity—as caught up by its very existence in a tremendous, dynamic movement of divine creative love. God's purpose is the flowing of this love from the Divine Trinity across all the eons of history, gradually filling all creation, until God is "all in all" (1 Cor. 15:28). This love is fully released into creation through the death and resurrection of Jesus Christ, as the Spirit of the Risen Jesus re-creates everyone and everything into the transparent embodiment of nothing but this love; finally, when the Lord Jesus comes again, the universe itself will be freed from the shackles of mortality and enter upon the liberty and splendor of the children of God (Rom. 8:21).

Within this faith vision, a human life and all human action find ultimate meaning. Thus, the Principle and Foundation rec-

ognizes that all of one's desires must be ordered to the fulfillment of God's loving design, and that all of one's use of creatures must be guided by the demands of living this love. The
length of time to be spent on praying the Principle and Foundation will depend upon the operative intensity of this faith vision
within the particular retreatant, since it is the beginning and
basis for the entire dynamic movement of the Exercises.[1] This
movement is directed toward helping the retreatant to be graced
with the effective desire always to choose and do that which will
most fulfill God's creative purpose, that is, always, in every action "to praise, reverence, and serve God our Lord." Living out
this faith vision of all reality day by day is to live discernment.
It is to find God in all things.

Dry as the language of Ignatius may seem in the text of
the Principle and Foundation, the origin of this vision as the
basis of his own life was the great illumination that he received
on the banks of the River Cardoner at Manresa.[2] His own experience of living the Spiritual Exercises was initiated by and
grounded in this illumination.

The first three paragraphs of the Principle and Foundation
enunciate a general theological principle: the fundamental faith
vision of all of reality. For many retreatants, the first series of

---

1.   A superb theological treatment of the objective faith vision of God's
purpose in creating all reality, which is the beginning and basis of all human
response to God, is given by Gilles Cusson, S.J., in his *Pedagogie de
l'experience spirituelle personnelle* (Paris: DDB, 1968), pp. 67-102.

2.   See my *Making an Apostolic Community of Love: The Role of the
Superior According to St. Ignatius of Loyola* (St. Louis: The Institute of Jesuit
Sources, 1970) pp. 20-21. For a thorough synthesis of the world view of
Ignatius expressed in the Principle and Foundation and underlying the entire
Spiritual Exercises and also the spirit of the Society of Jesus, see *The
Constitutions of the Society Of Jesus,* trans. George E. Ganss, S.J., with an
Introduction and a Commentary (St. Louis: The Institute of Jesuit Sources,
1970), pp. 3-32. See also his Editor's Foreword in *Jesuit Religious Life Today*
(St. Louis: The Institute of Jesuit Sources, 1977, pp. 17-20, especially pp. 19
and 20).

meditations may need to be focused simply on the reality of God.[3] Graced with this realization, one can be moved on to prayer on God's purpose in creating, revealed in the Bible as God's promise to enter into covenant with God's people, to share the divine life with all people—with me. Since this is the promise of God, it is an absolute promise of unending divine fidelity.

However, covenant is never actual until it is mutual. Therefore, God's promise is necessarily at the same time a call to God's people—to me—to respond to this call with total fidelity, the "praise, reverence, and service," which is to live love in all my actions. The instrument of fulfillment of God's promise is all creation. Everything that *is* is intended to be a vehicle of mutual, loving communication between God and human beings. The call to respond to the promise of God, then, is the call to live love, in all of one's actual relationships to everyone and everything that enters into one's life. Concretely, this means to use creatures insofar as they take one to God and to let them go insofar as they keep one from God.

The third and fourth paragraphs of the Principle and Foundation enunciate a practical principle concerning the response of a person to this fundamental faith vision of all reality. In order to live out totally a faithful response to the promise/call of God, Ignatius says that we "must make ourselves indifferent." This means that we must come to an interior attitude of complete openness to whatever God might use as a means to give Godself to us. To be indifferent is to recognize that God can use anything to do this. It is to be totally spiritually free—not holding on to any little boxes marked "private," not telling God that any particular way of coming to me is unacceptable, or that God can ask me to let anything go in order to go to God except *that*. To make ourselves indifferent is to open ourselves to the light of

---

3. See Appendix 1 in Part IV for a list of appropriate Scripture texts.

the Holy Spirit so that the Spirit can expose our idols here and now, and with gifted strength, to smash them.

Ignatius, then, supposes an active and ongoing *making* ourselves indifferent as we face here-and-now choices. This was misunderstood by St. Frances de Sales, whose interpretation was that a person has to come to a habitual disposition of indifference, a misinterpretation later exploited by the Quietists. Ignatius, rather, supposes that one has very strong desires, both interiorly and bodily. A person makes self indifferent when surrendering all one's desires to the concrete call of God that has already been discovered or will yet be discovered through the election [169-189]. Thus, a person will continually order all desires and choices to the praise and reverence and service of God, the decision will always be given to the truly spiritual desire, which is the movement of the Holy Spirit within one here and now.[4]

The faith vision of all reality of the Principle and Foundation, leading us to the profound interior liberty of always making ourselves indifferent, will bring among all the conflicting desires that an individual experiences the ruling desire simply to go to God, no matter what the cost. Thus, what I really want will always be to respond, "Yes, God," in all my concrete choices and actions here and now.

Gaston Fessard has summed up the vision of the Principle and Foundation excellently:

> "In the eyes of Ignatius there is the human person's own 'I' facing the Divine Majesty, and between them a world created uniquely in order that this 'I' perceive *there* the presence of a Sovereign Freedom calling one to God's service in order to

---

4. Cf. Gaston Fessard, S.J., *La Dialectique des Exercices Spirituels de Saint Ignace De Loyola*, Vol. I (Paris: Aubier, 1956). He points out, "The four weeks and the methods of Election have as their unique purpose to dispose us to receive each time the particular grace we need to live the Foundation here and now." p. 317 (my trans.).

give God in everything and through everything the greatest glory and praise."[5]

The stress in the Principle and Foundation is on the transcendence of God calling a person to order all desires and choices to the Divine service. The stress in the Contemplation to Attain Love of God [230-237] will be on the immanence of God inviting one to total mutual self-giving.

When going through the Exercises, it is well for the director to point out to the retreatant how the Principle and Foundation recurs repeatedly in the preparatory prayer [46], in the motive for choices [15], [179], [184], [189], [332], [342], and in the *agere contra* method to come to freedom [16], [157], [350]. The grace of the Principle and Foundation is shaped for a particular individual by the discernment of vocational calls from God already completed—one's personal vocation from God, in and through the Church, experienced as the call of the Spirit within oneself to mission, with one's companions as lay person or religious or priest—to be lived out now by ordering all one's desires and choices and actions to God.

When it becomes evident that the faith vision of all reality of the Principle and Foundation is operative in the consciousness of the retreatant, and the director does recognize as given the initial grace of effective desire both for total interior freedom and also the ruling desire always to live love, then the First Week of the Exercises can begin.

Moving Into the First Principle and Foundation [23]

When the retreatant exhibits an awareness of "all is gift," the director recognizes his or her readiness for the text of the Exercises, specifically that of the First Principle and Foundation.

---

5. Ibid., p. 354 (my trans.).

Although Ignatius does not assign actual prayer periods for this particular text, it must be considered well by the retreatant and responded to because it stands as the basis for all the prayer that follows.

Having spent some unstructured time during the preparation days in tuning up one's senses and in assuming a stance of receptivity to God and God's love, the retreatant will have brought into focus his or her own personal salvation history and will have arrived at some experiential knowledge of being loved gratuitously by God. Almost certainly the individual will also have moved into structured prayer, that is, spending an hour over a text of Scripture three or four times in a day.

So, now it is time for the direct consideration of the First Principle and Foundation. Some directors do this through Scripture, designating four prayer periods corresponding to the four sections of the First Principle and Foundation. When assigning a Scripture passage to be prayed over, the director indicates its purpose to the retreatant by putting a paragraph of the First Principle and Foundation in his or her own words, but without yet referring the retreatant to the text of the Exercises.

One passage from each of the following groupings might be given for each prayer period. These are only some suggested Scripture passages among many possible ones.

First Period

Gen. 1	First account of Creation: why were human beings created at all?
Ps. 8	What is a human being, that you are mindful of this individual?
Ezek. 16:3-14	God says to me: "Live." "The glory of God is one fully alive." (St. Irenaeus)
1 Cor. 3:21-23	You are Christ's and Christ is God's.

Second Period

Ps. 104	The glories of creation. This might be prayed outdoors, the retreatant recalling the tuning up of the senses from the first days.
Job 38:3-21	Poetic challenge to know that God is creator of all things.
Sir. 16:22-17:27	God's wisdom in creation.

Third Period

Gen. 2	Harmony in creation: creation is given to Adam for the use of human beings, for their care.
Deut. 30:11-14	The word of God is in your heart.
1 Kings 19:9-14	Asking for clearer vision: not everything reveals the Lord to us.
1 Cor. 10:23	All things are lawful, but not all things are good for us.

Fourth Period

Deut. 30:15-20	Choose life!
Eccles. 3	A time for everything
Phil. 3:7-14	All I want is to know Christ.
Phil. 2:1-11	Christ did not cling. This is a good passage for someone who seems to cling to honor.
Heb. 10:32-39	Remember what you have endured? This passage can be helpful for someone who has suffered and has become somewhat closed.

After the retreatant has spent at least a day praying over the Scripture in the manner mentioned above, the director gives the text from Ignatius and asks the retreatant to interpret what it means. When satisfied that the individual grasps its meaning, the director tells him or her to read it over several times in the day and to see if there is a deepening in a "yes" to its various parts.

Sometimes a retreatant has to grapple with its parts, like Jacob wrestling with the angel. If one cannot say yes to all of it by the end of the day, is there at least the desire to come to an ability to say a genuine yes? If the desire is not there, the director continues to give passages about the same things, especially passages about God's great love, letting God draw the retreatant through the words of Scripture.

The struggle toward indifference, an expected dynamic that must be entered into, reveals some of the greatest areas of unfreedom for an individual. Too facile a yes must be avoided, but the retreatant should be manifesting a genuine movement toward a desire for indifference and the call to the "more" of the last sentence. It is that desire which indicates one's readiness to proceed into the First Week of the Exercises.

The *Spiritual Exercises*, while very contemporary, were written in the language of the sixteenth century. An interesting challenge in our day is to change the sexist vocabulary without altering the meaning of Ignatius. In reading the First Principle and Foundation with this change, one is confronted with a much broader reality than is immediately evident in the translations of the text currently extant. "Man is created . . ." might easily be limited to "this man" or "woman," or even to "I am created . . ." Indeed, saying "*We* are created to praise, reverence, and serve God . . ." provides a different vision.

To be true, then, to the collective nature of the word "we," the opening sentence of the First Principle and Foundation should not culminate in ". . . and by this means to save our souls," as if this is done in isolation, but rather ". . . and by this means to save all humankind." This kind of vocabulary emphasizes the communal nature of salvation and the interdependence of all persons. This is especially true regarding the resources of the earth. All the other things on the face of the earth have been given to all of us to lead us to this end. Insofar as they help in the attainment of this end, namely the salvation of all humankind, we make use of them; otherwise not.

As the director gets to know the retreatant in these early days of the retreat, he or she can assess whether or not this social dimension should be highlighted. Is the retreatant from an affluent country that uses all "the other things on the face of the earth" as if they were the exclusive property of that nation? Is there oppression of other people for the attainment of more resources? Does the retreatant have an appreciation of the social nature of stewardship over the world and its goods? What happens to the notion of indifference if it affects the "good life" one is used to within a particular social milieu?

Is the retreatant from a developing country or from an oppressed people, deprived by others from a just share in the world's goods? How does this reality affect this retreatant's approach to indifference?

Directors themselves should live in an awareness of these realities and gently but firmly expand the horizons of any retreatant who is too content to live, think, and pray within very narrow limits. The director who ignores this social dimension, especially within the First Principle and Foundation, may be failing to confront the retreatant with the full apostolic nature of the Exercises.

On the other hand, the director must always be aware of the directive of Ignatius to remain "as a balance at equilibrium"[15]. Thus, the director includes the social dimension without making the Exercises into a platform for expressing his or her own views on the world order. Specific allusion to the social dimension at the early stages of the retreat should render unnecessary continued repetition of this aspect as the retreat progresses. It is the work of the Holy Spirit, not of the director, to move the retreatant.

Chapter 3

The First Week

Dynamics of the First Week [24-90]

In this section I will first discuss the underlying meaning of each portion of the First Week, in its order of occurrence, and then I will provide some considerations on prayer within the Exercises, especially during the First Week.

Introduction of the First Week [24-44]

In continuity with a tradition of Christian spirituality going back to the Fathers of the Desert, Ignatius recognizes the central importance of the twice daily examination of conscience as the chief means of living a discerning life day by day and of growing toward finding God in all things. Thus, before beginning the exercises of the First Week, he presents a method for daily particular examination of conscience [24-31] and general examination of conscience [32-43], as well as a preparation for general confession and holy communion [44].[1] The particular examination of conscience is an excellent means of focusing one's operational attitudes toward daily fidelity to the call of God discovered in one's election.

---

1. Some directors prefer to postpone the material concerning preparation for confession to the time within the exercises of the First Week, in order to make certain that the retreatant has a healthy, biblical sense of sin. See the explanation that introduces the Second Exercise [55-61].

Following the tradition, Ignatius proposes five points for the general examination: (1) giving thanks to God for favors received; (2) asking grace to know my sins and rid myself of them; (3) examination of my response to God; (4) act of contrition; (5) purpose of amendment. Because of an unfortunate confessional catechesis and the style of pedagogy proposing the examination of conscience, many people in recent times have experienced the fivefold schema as formalistic, and not a few have dropped the practice of examination altogether. Thus, the director may find it necessary to show the retreatant the vital importance of this daily exercise and help one to make it well.

Many people find it helpful to change the terminology to "consciousness examen," emphasizing that the process is not introspective searching through an objective list of faults to pinpoint one's own guilt, but rather allowing to rise spontaneously to consciousness the way that one has been sensitive to God's presence in people, events, and situations during the half-day, and how one has failed to respond to God's presence, against the backdrop of God's personal love—specifically as experienced during the half-day seen during the thanksgiving moments.[2] This approach recaptures the ancient Christian meaning of conscience, expressed by Cassian as "the transparency of the spirit before God."

Another help to restore this central practice of prayer for ongoing growth in discernment is recognition that the five traditional steps in the method are not the results of formalistic theory, but the fruit of reflected-upon experience of great Christians at the origins of Christian spirituality. On reflection, one finds that these five steps actually are the five successive moments in any dynamic movement of personal love: what we always want to say to a person whom we truly love, in the order in which we want to say it.[3]

---

2. See the excellent article by George Aschenbrenner, S.J., "Consciousness Examen," *Review for Religious*, vol. 31 (Jan. 1972), p. 14.

1. "Thank you." When we offer our love to another we take the terrible risk of having it rejected. When a person, that tremendous mystery of freedom, returns our love, our first and spontaneous response is one of gratitude for this great gift.

2. "Help me." Next, we feel our own inadequacy to respond to such a gift, and, out of this poverty, we ask for help to become sensitive to the ways that we do and do not respond.

3. "I love you." As our response and lack of response rises spontaneously to consciousness, we find ourselves saying, "I do really love you, in spite of the weakness and failure in my response."

4. "I'm sorry." Awareness of our failure to respond, in spite of the sincerity of our love, is expressed by true sorrow.

5. "Be with me." We end with the ruling desire of every true lover, wanting the beloved to be with one, helping one to respond ever more authentically to the gift of love.

So in the examination of conscience, we want to say to God:

1. "Thank you, God . . . How great you are!" And we allow to rise to consciousness all God's specific gifts of this half-day, all the ways that God has become present to us through people and events and situations.

2. "Help me." In the light of God's gifts, we begin to be aware of how insensitive to God's presence we have been, how blind, how deaf. We pray that God will help us to see and to hear.

3. "But I do love you, God." And the ways that we have been blind and deaf during this half-day arise spontaneously into awareness. When one is in love, there is no need to search through an objective list of possible faults to become aware

---

3. I am indebted to Richard M. Rice, S.J., for sharing this insight with me.

of how one has failed to love. So, we become conscious of the ways that we have missed God's presence and not responded to God.

4. "I'm sorry." This is not a depressing moment, but a moment of Eucharist: from thanksgiving through contrition to communion. "Lord, I am not worthy." But, like the father of the Prodigal Son, God is still inviting us to a party.

Kiss me Jesus. I won't do it again. Thérèse

5. "Be with me, God . . . With your grace, I shall love you better during this next half day."

Thus, in the examination of conscience, a person plays back the half-day to see his or her response: Whom have I loved? What have I loved? Did I respond to God in all that I did?

This exercise works in an ongoing way on one's decisiveness in choosing among multiple goods, and gradually transforms the attitudes that a person is living out of, so that responses to God will be ever more discerning. One becomes, day by day, more sensitive to God's presence and more responsive to God in every person, every event, every thing. It is well to point out to the retreatant Ignatius' definition of perfection, which is finding God in all things:

> The perfect, due to constant contemplation and the enlightenment of the understanding, consider, meditate, and ponder more that God our Lord is in every creature by His essence, power, and presence [39].

The twice daily examination of conscience helps one grow more and more toward finding God in all things.

The Exercises of the First Week [45-72]

The "points" given by Ignatius within each exercise place us before the Church's objective understanding of sin. First of all, it is necessary to place ourselves before this objective understanding, to which we shall respond personally according to the movements of the Holy Spirit within us. Yes, the objective element always controls the subjective element. *Intuitives?*

The exercises of the First Week are designed to bring the retreatant to the realization of being a sinner in a world of sin: Am I going to reinforce the world of sin in myself and in the Church and in humanity, or am I going to struggle against it? Profound awareness of sin will enable me to better comprehend the weight of sinfulness upon my interior liberty and its obscuring of my spiritual insight and its weakening of my desire for God above all other desires.[4] Thus, it will bring me to open myself to be freed and healed by Christ—to stand defenseless before the gratuity of God's love.

In our times, it is important that a director be aware of the structural weight of social sin in the world and help the retreatant to grow in this awareness and in freedom from an unconscious acculturation into cooperation with or lack of sensitivity to this dimension of evil. Although this handbook is not designed to develop in detail that dimension in directing the Exercises, it is necessary for a director to stress the reality of one's reinforcing the world of social sin in humanity.[5]

First Exercise [45-53]

I pray for the grace of "shame and confusion"—shame, in that I do reinforce the sinfulness of the world by my own sins; and confusion, insofar as the absurdity and unreality of sin, in

---

4. The director often will need to explain the Rules for the Discernment of Spirits during the First Week [8], [9], [314-327]. See "Rules for Discernment of Spirits I" in Part III.

5. See an excellent treatment by José Magaña, S.J., *Ignatian Pre-Exercises and Theology: A Spirituality for Liberation* (St. Louis: Institute of Jesuit Sources, 1977). See also Michael J. O'Sullivan, S.J., "Towards a Social Hermeneutic of the Spiritual Exercises with an Application to the Annotations" (Master's thesis, Jesuit School of Theology at Berkeley, California, 1979), a first-rate study of this dimension.

light of the Principle and Foundation [23], give rise to stupor
and astonishment. The focus here is not on the kind or the gravity of my sins, but upon their number; hence, the constant reflection in each of the points is on my many sins in the light of
the results of one sin, all in order that I may be open to receive
the grace of "shame and confusion"[48].

1. *First Point* [50]. Through the experience of the Principle
   and Foundation [23], I have come to realize that "all is
   gift." Meditation upon the sin of the angel shows that sin
   essentially is not wanting to receive God's gift. It is to
   "lack Eucharist." St. Gregory of Nyssa compares the angels
   to mirrors and, thus, explains the origin of evil:

   > A mirror receiving the image of the sun and transmitting
   > this light to other mirrors becomes aware of its own de-
   > pendence on the source of light. It refuses, then, to re-
   > ceive from the source, because it wants *itself* to be for
   > itself and for others the only source of light. Conse-
   > quently, it becomes dark.

   Here then, in the Spiritual Exercises begins the great struggle between light and darkness that will climax in the meditation on Two Standards [136-148] and in the Third Week
   [190-209] and the Fourth Week [218-229]. The Principle
   and Foundation [23] revealed all creation as a tremendous,
   dynamic movement of light whose origin is God. With the
   sin of the angels, a tremendous counter-movement of darkness is initiated: the Satanic dynamic straining to overcome
   the Christ dynamic in the world through social sin and in
   each individual person through personal sin.

   My own many sins have strengthened the movement of
   darkness. This realization opens me to receive the grace of
   "shame and confusion" [48].

2. *Second Point* [51]. The entrance of the movement of darkness into the earth—Original Sin—is experienced by a per-

son as the sinful condition of the world into which each is born—an ever-widening movement of darkness through the ages because of personal sins compounding social sin through sinful political and economic structures which bring about social evils of dispersion, disunity, disorder, and injustice.

My own many sins have widened the movement of darkness, so, I pray to be gifted with "shame and confusion" [48].

3. *Third Point* [52]. The consequence of freely and definitively choosing the darkness in one total personal act is to put oneself into hell. Ignatius points here not necessarily to a fact of an individual in hell, but rather to the real possibility of this happening because of the real meaning of real mortal sin. He does this in order to complete the logic of the dynamic of comparing my many sins to the results of one sin, in order that I may open myself to receive the grace of "shame and confusion" [48].

4. *Colloquy* [53]. This looking long at Jesus on the cross for my sins provides the backdrop for the rest of the whole First Week. It makes utterly clear the response of God to sin manifested in the pierced Heart of Jesus, the Word made flesh. The Father enters into the world of sin in helplessness through the body of His Son in order to save us (Phil. 2:5-9).

"What ought I to do for Christ?"

The First Week looks not only to the past, but also to the future.

5. *Note on Colloquies* [54-61]. "Speaking exactly as one friend speaks to another," I am to express the feelings flowing from the graced insights of the prayer period. Thus Ignatius introduces the colloquy, a form of prayer that is very dear to him. The director should help anyone unacquainted with

this familiar and loving way of speaking to the Lord to grow toward doing it with ease.

Second Exercise [55]

Now, against the backdrop of the reality and the majesty as well as the unending love and fidelity of the all good God, who created the entire universe as a means to share divine life with all human persons—with me, I contemplate the reality of my own salvation history, which begins with the reality of my own sins. Experiencing the personal love relationship into which God has called me, I pray to come to a true understanding of my own sinfulness and brokenness in response to God's gifting, and, so, to a "growing and intense sorrow and tears for my sins" [55]. This sorrow, however, is always felt in the radical peace of the experience of the reality of God's love for me *nevertheless*—his forgiving, saving love embodied in the pierced Heart of Jesus. I am a sinner, but a sinner infinitely loved by God.

Preparing a retreatant to do this exercise may require correcting his or her catechesis on confession. What is sought is not compiling a moralistic list of sins, but coming to a global awareness of my sinfulness during my life.[6] One must overcome a legalistic approach to sin, in order to have the biblical understanding of sin as the breaking of a personal relationship of love.

Thus, I do not measure objective "mortal" or "venial" sins, but rather my own breaking of my own personal relationship of love with God. The evil of the sin is proportionate to the gifts of God's personal love to me. This is why Teresa of Avila could sincerely feel herself to be "the greatest of sinners." It is why Peter's sin was worse than that of Judas. So too, patricide is seen to be worse than homicide, even though both are objectively murder. We "good people" who make retreats must over-

---

6. An application of the principles given by Ignatius in Some Notes on Scruples [345-351] can be helpful for some retreatants here.

come our unconscious pharisaical attitude—"Thank you, Lord, that I am not as sinful as others"—and come to experience the insight of Job: "I was a fool. Now I have seen your face. I repent in dust and ashes" (Job 42:1-4).

The dynamic of the Spiritual Exercises beginning with the First Principle and Foundation [23] brings the retreatant first to look at God and, only then, at sin in the light of God. To know myself as a sinner is to grow in the knowledge of the loving, faithful God. Thus, I can look head on at my sinfulness knowing that I am a loved sinner. God loves me nevertheless, just as I am! Consequently, I can love myself and I can let others love me, in spite of everything. This is why the atmosphere of this exercise should be one of deep peace and gratitude.

The dynamic of the second exercise moves forward as a great dialogue with God, like that of Job with the Creator. I ask for a growing intense sorrow and for tears of compunction to break the hardness of my heart as rock is broken into sand. This is a gift only God can give, as Father Laplace points out; and God gives it in ways that we do not expect.

1. *First Point* [56]. This is a global review of my salvation history within my human biography, seeing whatever sins rise to my memory under the movement of the Holy Spirit. The purpose is to grasp my own sinfulness, the movement of darkness within me which I actualize each time I sin. When I sin, I thrust myself into the mystery of iniquity, the Satanic dynamic of darkness. I reinforce the sinfulness of the world. I affirm my own being as refusal of God's gift, breaking my personal relationship of love with God.

2. *Second Point* [57]. The "gravity" of my sins, here, does not refer to "mortal" or "venial" sins as such, but to the evil of deepening the Satanic dynamic of darkness in myself and in the world through my refusal to respond to God's love. Ignatius mentions "mortal sin" because he was writing out of

his own experience, and he was conscious of many of these in his own life.

The purpose of this prayer is to be graced with a growing sorrow for my sins [55].

3. *Third Point* [58]. The dynamic of growing sorrow deepens by situating myself within all creation before God and realizing that to sin is to want to be left to myself—only myself.

The "corruption and loathsomeness of my body" is not some kind of puritanical contempt of the flesh, but rather the concrete recognition of the consequences of sin within my own body-person and upon the collective sinfulness of the world.

Finally, I am "a source of corruption and contagion" because by my sins I have reinforced the social sinfulness of the human community, and I have caused the holy Church to be the sinful Church by making myself a diseased cell in the Mystical Body of Christ. It is helpful to invite the retreatant here to see the faces of persons who have been led away from God through contact with oneself.

4. *Fourth Point* [59]. The dynamic of growing insight and feeling increases through deeper understanding of the meaning of my sins, resulting in "growing and intense sorrow." Here, I look at the loving, faithful God whom I experienced in the Principle and Foundation [23], and also at the sinful self whom I have come to know more deeply through the dynamic progression of the previous points.

This is the climax of the dialogue of Job with God: "Holy, Holy, You are always Holy. I repent in dust and ashes" (Job 42:1-6).

5. *Fifth Point* [60]. The dynamic of this exercise now flows into the "cry of wonder," which became a deep mystical

experience in the saints. I surround myself with the world's body—God's creation—experiencing God's faithful love still coming to me through creatures: I am loved in spite of everything.

It is good to invite the retreatant also to reflect that one among all of these creatures, namely, the Church, the Mystical Body of Christ, is praying for me and is constantly accepting the Spirit of God into the world for me. No matter what sins I commit, the Church never gives up on me but still loves me—nevertheless!

6. *Colloquy* [61]. This exercise ends, then, in peaceful gratitude. It is good to contemplate here the mercy of God embodied in the pierced Heart of Jesus on the Cross, as was done in the first exercise. Because of the mercy of God, I am no longer closed in on myself. I am carried by the Love that creates me and recreates me. To "resolve . . . to amend for the future" means to open myself to Christ.

To say, "I am a sinner," is to say, "I need Jesus Christ."

Third Exercise [62-63]

The goal is, through repetition, to discern and to develop the orientation of insights and of feelings, as they manifest a continuity of the action of God in a retreatant. The grace to be sought is threefold [63]:

1. The "knowledge of my sins" sought here is not a natural knowledge derived from personal study, but a spiritual knowledge given by God. I desire to know the power of sin, of the Satanic dynamic within me (Rom. 5-7; Ps. 19:12-14).

2. The "understanding of the disorder of my actions" sought here means to understand the vital desires within me—for possessions, for honor, for life—which are rooted in human reality and, so, are basically good, but which resist the call of God to "live Christ" and which tend to seek independent

satisfaction. I pray for this understanding, so that I can "put my life in order" and have the positive vigilance to guard my re-found love.

3. The "knowledge of the world" is recognition of the sinful-ness of the world as the situation of the Satanic dynamic of darkness in history, so that I can put away from me any-thing opposed to the Christ dynamic of always moving to-ward God. It is recognition, too, of the acculturated blind-ness to social sin that leads me unconsciously to support sinful structures in the world. The prayer is: "Do not leave me in the power of my sins. Do not leave me to myself."

Father Laplace points out that the goal of the entire progres-sive dynamic of the First Week is to stand *naked* before God, not in order to be terrified at our nakedness, but in order to find God's love to be the only real security, a love that accepts us as we are, even while we are afraid to face and accept ourselves. Through this experience of God lov-ing me just as I am, I can come to love myself and to allow others to love me.

Fourth Exercise [64]
This is a prayerful synthesis of the orientation of the entire series of movements and of insights that the Lord has given to the retreatant through the preceding exercises of the First Week, with a profound praying for a deepening of these gifts.

Fifth Exercise [65-71]
Ignatius completes the movement of the Satanic dynamic of darkness by carrying it to its logical terminal point. He pro-poses a meditation on hell. His presentation is full of medieval imagery, which initially may turn off many contemporary retreatants. Nevertheless, experience has shown that the graces of this meditation are so valuable that the director should en-

deavor to redeem the imagery in order to help the retreatant to receive these graces.

Hell supposes one's own death—my ultimate "Yes" or "No" to God, prepared by all the choices that I have made during my life. Hell is the free ultimate determination of self, the sum of all my choices creating the absence of God. Hell is to be left *only* to myself. Yet, as a matter of fact, God is not absent from hell; rather, what one experiences is one's own total chosen alienation from God, finding oneself outside of God *in God,* in a mad turning in upon one's own nothingness. The "exterior darkness" exists within the damned person. St. Jude, in his letter, paints this powerfully: "rainless clouds driven before the wind, leafless trees without fruit, doubly dead and uprooted, wild sea waves foaming up their own shame, wandering stars doomed forever to utter darkness" (Jude 1:12-13).

The grace to be prayed for is a "deep sense of the pain which the lost suffer, that if because of my faults I forget the love of the eternal Lord, at least the fear of these punishments will keep me from falling into sin" [65-Second Prelude]. To pray for motives that can support the motive of the love of God in order to resist the force of disordered desires is a realistic approach that only the most romantic naive person would question. Teilhard de Chardin beautifully paraphrased this *id quod volo:*

> O, Jesus . . . I desire to make the ever present threat of damnation a part of my habitual and practical vision of the world, not in order to fear you, but in order to become more intensely yours.[7]

Ignatius' vision of hell in the first prelude [65] and in the five points of this exercise [66-70] is highly anthropomorphic; hence, very biblical. What he proposes is an "application of the

---

7. Teilhard de Chardin, Pierre, *The Divine Milieu* (New York: Harper and Brothres, 1960), p. 131.

senses," so that as body-person I can experience the situation of an individual made for union with God, but who would freely close self totally to God. Good psychologist that he was, Ignatius is helping the retreatant, through imagining psychosomatic suffering, to realize the consequences, when the whole thrust of the human person's being-toward-God is entirely frustrated; and, therefore, every part of the person is frustrated, including all the senses.

1. *First Point* [66]. The idea of hell fire is biblical and is a powerful symbol of total frustration.

2. *Second Point* [67]. The sense of hearing especially introduces the presence of others in a situation of complete alienation and mutual hate. In the absence of the Spirit, people are impenetrable to one another. Jean-Paul Sartre, in his play *No Exit,* put it, "Hell is other people."

3. *Third Point* [68]. The sense of smell mediates the chosen environment of evil.

4. *Fourth Point* [69]. Gerard Manley Hopkins, the Jesuit poet, expressed this pain with great force:

   > "On a rack, where self-wrung, self-strung,
   >   sheathe-and-shelterless,
   > Thoughts against thoughts in groans grind."

5. *Fifth Point* [70]. The burning of the fire, St. Thomas Aquinas reflected, is like an internal spontaneous combustion resulting from the free exclusion of God from self forever. Every faculty of the body-person is existentially ordered to union with God by creation. Just as beatitude will permeate the risen bodies of the saints, so damnation permeates the body: this is hell fire.

6. *Colloquy* [71]. Ignatius is very biblical here, introducing the entire sweep of salvation history, recalling that to put one-

self into hell is a risk of all human persons (Cf. [52]; [102]; [103]).

One can definitively reject God through the fundamental option of rejecting the gift of faith that "Jesus is Lord." Or believing, one can freely choose to act definitively against Christ's law of love. Recognizing this concrete risk of hell, the retreatant should be moved to fervent thanksgiving: not only have I not fallen into hell, but I have been forgiven and loved and protected by God. This meditation also ends in peaceful thanksgiving.

At the end of number 71, Ignatius inserts a remark about "Other Exercises" in parentheses. It is interesting that he does not suggest any meditations on the mercy of God, but rather "on death and other punishments of sin, on judgment, etc." Many directors do find it helpful to propose special meditations on the mercy of God, such as the Prodigal Son, during the First Week. Ignatius would seem to believe that the movements within the exercises that he gives, as well as the colloquies, would focus the retreatant powerfully on the awareness of God's loving forgiveness. An experienced director has suggested that, actually, Ignatius' own meditation on mercy is The Kingdom of Christ [91-98] wherein the response of Jesus to the retreatant, now profoundly aware of his or her own sinfulness and unworthiness, is not merely, "I forgive you," but the astonishing call, "You, sinner, labor with me to bring the Kingdom to be for the glory of my Father."

Next, Ignatius introduces a Note [72], which again shows his insistence on flexibility. The director must not become a slave to procedures as ends in themselves, but should maintain a great freedom within the framework of the Spiritual Exercises, according to the temperament and gifts of God to each retreatant.

Within that prevailing framework of flexibility, Ignatius does suggest in a brief, early document written to a Jesuit, probably Father Polanco, a manner of presenting the exercises of the First Week:

1. First, give the Foundation [23];

2. then, the Particular Examen [24-31];

3. then, the General Examen [32-42];

4. then, the Daily Examen with five points [43].

5. Afterwards, on the evening of the first day, if possible, propose the first exercise [45-54], so that the retreatant can begin to make it at midnight.

6. On the second day, in the morning propose the second exercise [55-61].

7. After the meal, give the third [62-63] and the fourth [64] at one time.

8. On the same second day, after supper, explain the Additions [73-90], so that the retreatant can use these with the first exercise at midnight and the other exercises on the third day: on rising, the second; before dinner, the third; the fourth after dinner; after Vespers, if possible, the fifth.

9. On the fourth day, begin at midnight. The second rising; the third after Mass; the fourth in the afternoon; the fifth after supper, if the one making the exercises is capable of this.

10. Afterwards, propose an examen over all the exercises. Begin to explain the Rules for the Discernment of Spirits in the First Week [313-327].

11. Always at the end present something new.[8]

Later on in the same document, Ignatius gives advice about what the director does during the direction session:

---

8. *Directoria Exercitiorum Spiritualium*, 1540-1599 (Rome: Historical Institute of the Society of Jesus, 1955), pp. 82-83.

1. Ask about the fruit sought in this exercise, for example, contrition.

2. If the retreatant responds well, it is not good to spend much time on that, nor to ask many other things.

3. If the retreatant did not fully obtain the fruit sought, then the director should diligently question one about movements, observance of the Additions, and so forth.

4. The director can also advise the retreatant to write down insights and movements experienced.[9]

In the remainder of this chapter, I treat some notions regarding prayer. Basic to the retreatant's prayer during thirty days is the stance before God affirmed through a consideration of the First Principle and Foundation [23], namely "to praise, reverence, and serve God our Lord." Such a stance reflects three central realities that pervade all authentic Christian prayer: (1) the reality of the one, true, Triune God who is love; (2) the reality of myself as a unique personal self-awareness ordered entirely to fulfillment in God; (3) the reality of my own place in continuing salvation history—the coming of God to meet me in Jesus Christ through his Church in my own specific Christian vocation at every moment.

I must have, then, the true and deep realization of the radical dependence of my own being upon God's creative love—my radical poverty. My consciousness of the absolute reality of God is what is meant by the "praise" of God, and my consciousness of my own absolute dependence upon God is what is meant by "reverence;" these are the loving adoration and the loving surrender that constitute the personal encounter with God which is prayer. This encounter is lived at every moment of my life in every concrete situation by my response to the actual word of God to me here and now, which I discern calling me to respond

9. *Ibid.*, p. 85.

in this way at this moment. It is thus that I "serve God our Lord" finding God in all things, praying always.

When I bring this encounter with God to the level of conscious awareness, I engage in formal prayer. I lay aside all other activities, and I concentrate my whole person upon being together with God. This is why when I go to formal prayer, I should do so with great eagerness, great joy, and great naturalness. As I approach the prayer, my thought should be: "I am going to meet God; I am going to have a personal encounter with my one great Love."

It is in the light of this that we should understand the ongoing Preparatory Prayer [46], [49], the Preludes [47], [48], [49], and the Additional Directions [73-90] of Ignatius. A person composes self to pray by gathering up the scattered forces of mind, imagination, feelings, body, so that one's whole self will be there for this loving encounter with God. However, these procedures do not mean that an individual should strain through some kind of artificial ritual, as if certain words and gestures would have a magical effect upon prayer. No, one must go to God naturally in the way that is real now for him or her.

If I truly realize the meaning of the reality of God and of my own absolute dependence upon creative love, my own radical poverty, I shall establish a basic, existential attitude that spontaneously will react to the thought, "I am going to meet God." If I really have the sense of God, a lived sense of God that has seized my very being, I shall recoil into my own dependence, my own unique springing up from nothingness as an act of God's love; and, quite spontaneously, I shall be reverent in the deepest way, because I shall be *living* humility, true poverty. And this prayer will penetrate my whole life with the profound peace of one who lives in God and finds God in all things.

> See, I am God. See, I am all thing. See, I do all thing. See, I never lift my hands off my works, nor ever shall without end. See, I lead all thing to the end I ordained it to without begin-

ning; by the same might, wisdom and love whereby I made it.
How should anything be amiss? (from *Julian of Norwich*)

An essential preparation for prayer is the practice tradition-
ally called recollection. Now, just as it is necessary to find one's
own way of praying, so it is necessary to find one's own way of
recollection—the turning of one's whole self toward the service
of God: not being double-minded, not dissipated, not spilled out.

To establish this kind of personal recollection requires a
real fidelity to interior movements of the Holy Spirit, allowing
the continuity of insights and feelings to polarize all one's forces around the desire to serve God. Recollection involves col-
lecting together all of one's faculties, bringing them "into line,"
so that the fundamental commitment to God through Christ can
pass into act here and now.

Every individual, because of personal temperament and
past sins and failures and because of basic weakness and brokenness, has formed habits on various psychological and bodily
levels that intervene to hinder the movements of the Spirit from
passing into act and put an obstacle between God's word calling
this way here and now and one's response. This pattern of habits
precisely reveals in each person one's own personal area for
self-abnegation: for interior pacification and liberation.

Someone will experience, for example, the call to stop a
flow of egotistic daydreaming, or of bitter resentment, or of jeal-
ousy or of discouragement, or of desires running away from the
service of God. What is aimed at in the practice of recollection
is a *formed* tendency of one's desires—all of them, all this force
—toward the constant service of God and, therefore, toward an
ever deeper taste for prayer.

Recollection is the effort to make a profound turning of the
self at its root toward God, in order to allow God to mark, mod-
ify and shape the self, as it is already marked, modified, and
shaped by sin. It is an interior liberation, so that whatever I do

will be the concrete actualization here and now of my response to God through my specific Christian vocation.

The entire dynamic of the Spiritual Exercises is that of a progressive deepening of prayer—of the conscious experience of the presence of God within self, in order continually to recognize God's presence in everyone and everything and so, to live discernment. Prayer is the conscious exercise of faith and hope in God's word, of waiting for God and listening to God, and of recognizing God's coming as sometimes happens to all of us, if we let it, in a moment of great light or a moment of great joy.

Ignatius offers the Preludes [47], [48], [49] simply as aids to enter into prayer, to orient my whole being and all of my powers toward God. Otherwise, I shall engage only in reflection, not in prayer. In the first exercise of the First Week, Ignatius introduces the retreatant to a prayer method using the three faculties of memory, understanding, and will [50].[10] Karl Rahner translates these faculties as "the spirit in its self-presence, in its self-intuition, and in its self-activity."[11]

I confront my *me*, all that I carry within my consciousness of myself known in faith, from study and from experience. I go over this knowledge in my present consciousness, not by intellectual analysis, but by reflecting upon it—making comparisons and considering examples and implications in order to clarify my understanding. In the light of this understanding, I choose God and I affirm my choice in prayer. I allow the Spirit of God to shape me into who I really am.

This remembering and reflecting should lead me to profound acts of choosing God freely, responding to God's presence and God's reality, God's action in my own sacred history,

---

10. The Spiritual Exercises are a school of prayer as well as of discernment, and Ignatius provides a remarkable variety of methods of prayer in his text. Cf. [24-31]; [43]; [45-53]; [62-63]; [65-71]; [101-109]; [118]; [121]; [203-237]; [238-260].

11. Rahner, Karl, S.J., *Spiritual Exercises*, trans. Kenneth Baker, S.J., (New York: Herder and Herder, 1965), p. 43.

by resting in deep, felt attitudes of praise, thanksgiving, contrition, and so on. There where I find God, I rest and return.

Julian of Norwich expressed it well:

> I saw God and I sought God, and I had God and I wanted God. And this should be our common experience, as to my sight. . . . For God will be seen, and God will be sought; God will be awaited, and God will be trusted.

Since the prayer of the Exercises is very personal, it is well to recall that *no* Christian prayer is truly private prayer. Rather, it is the prayer of Christ realized within us by the Holy Spirit. To pray is a gift of God. Our prayer is Christ's prayer realized in his Church. Thus, it identifies us with the life of the whole People of God. Therefore, it is never individual. The prayer of the Spiritual Exercises is meant to help me to become who I really am—to become free to serve Christ always. This service is realized by a Christian precisely in the service of other people, bringing the Kingdom to be in the mutual relationships of all human persons and in the social structures that organize these relationships. However, just as in Ignatius' image of bodily exercise, only I can build up the strength of my own body, so, ultimately only I can offer myself to the Holy Spirit to be transformed for the service of others [1]; (cf. [5], [6], [12], [13], [16], [18]). I do this through freely choosing to be totally open to the director [17] and through generously giving myself to the prayer of the Exercises.

A Prayer During the First Week

I pray that the God of our Lord Jesus Christ,
> the all glorious Father/Mother God,
give me spiritual powers of wisdom and vision,
> by which there comes knowledge of God,
that my inward eyes may be illumined,
> so that I may know the hope to which

God calls me. . . .
the wealth and glory God offers me
among God's People,
and the vast resources of God's power
open to me
trusting in God. (cf. Eph. 1:17-19)

Moving Into the First Week [24-90]

When the director perceives that the retreatant has the necessary dispositions of gratitude for God's great love and of desire for indifference [23], it is time to move into the First Week. The conference is liable to last the full hour, since there is much to explain on the first day: (1) the dynamic of the week, not preempting the graces to be given, however; (2) how to make an Ignatian meditation; (3) the additional directions; (4) the particular examen.

Because it is almost certain that a retreatant will spend more than one day in the First Week, there are two major ways that directors present this material, depending on the director and the retreatant.

1. Following Ignatius as he presents it in the *Spiritual Exercises*, some directors give all the matter concerning sin on the first day of the First Week. If the grace of the week is not experienced by the retreatant, the following days are spent in five exercises, but with the use of Scripture that will help dispose the retreatant for that grace.

2. Other directors divide the material, feeling it is too much and too heavy for one day. In this instance Scripture texts will usually provide the basis for prayer. An example of this latter method follows.

The First Day

In introducing the First Week the director provides the retreatant with an underlying explanation, first pointing out that the retreatant has been getting deeply in touch with God's great, merciful, and gratuitous love. He or she has felt the call to a free response to God and an indifference to all that is not God, with a growing desire for a deepening of that indifference. Now it is time for the retreatant to begin looking at the disorder, the sinfulness, into which all of us have been born and which is so much a part of us. It is this disorder that gets in the way of indifference. Today the retreatant will pray over this disorder and sin as it came into the world, not yet concentrating on one's own personal sin.

Meditating on sin as it came into the world includes the present reality: What about the social evils of our day and how each of us participates in them, encourages them, or simply accepts them without a struggle? The retreatant is part of a culture, a social entity that is not always just toward others. Through prayer the person can own the social sinfulness of which he or she is a part and stand before our loving God who is aware of all the abuse God's children inflict on one another. Addiction to comfort or blindness to social evil is part of the disorders a retreatant should be led to face.

All too often the notion of personal sin is too narrow and petty. God's perspective is so much broader than ours, as is God's perspective on salvation. The director tries to assist the retreatant to see sin and salvation from God's vantage point and to give an appropriate response. Perhaps all the retreatant can do is mourn as one who is, indeed, part of a sinful social structure, and thus come to understand by experience that "blessed are those who mourn."

Ignatius suggests five exercises each day of this week, among them a midnight meditation. This does not mean the hour called "midnight," but rather a prayer period situated in the middle of the night. This has proved to be very grace-filled for many people and is worth a try. Some retreat directors will suggest that the retreatant not set an alarm, but ask God, before going to sleep, to awaken him or her if and when God wants to meet the retreatant in prayer. This relieves the retreatant of anxiety and also gives the courage to rise and pray. Other directors will ask the retreatant to set an alarm for three hours after retiring so that the first deep sleep is past. The isolation of this hour when one rises solely to be with the Lord and goes back to sleep afterward lends a precious quality to it and often it is the time for special grace. Explaining this, the director asks the retreatant to attempt the midnight meditation, unless health reasons would not warrant it.

First Prayer Period

Here one prays over the first sin as it came into creation, the sin of the angels [50]. If Scripture is desired for this exercise, the director might suggest one of the following: 2 Pet. 2:4, Rev. 12:113:18, and Rev. 20:7-10.

It is in presenting this meditation that a director will usually go into detail about the structure Ignatius suggests for this type of prayer [45-49], [53], [77]. Some retreat directors prefer explaining this form of prayer without using the text, so the retreatant will not feel overcome by the terms "Preparatory Prayer, Preludes, Points, and Colloquy" and get so concentrated on these things that the structure gets in the way rather than serves.

Using words similar to the following, the director shows the simple movement of the prayer period:

Now let me explain to you how to go about these exercises. They will be different from the kind of prayer you have been doing. These are Ignatian meditations. Some of the things I say will apply to every prayer period for the rest of the retreat, but I will use the first exercise, on the sin of the angels, as a model for you.

1. As you move to your place of prayer, stand there for a moment or two and realize what it is you are about to do. Also know that God awaits this time with you and has special grace in store for you. Then take your place with great reverence [75].

2. As you begin any prayer period, ask for the grace that everything you do, especially this prayer, will be for God's greater honor and glory [46]. Today's theme is an understanding of sin from God's point of view. Ask God, therefore, for the grace of proper response; in the context of this prayer period ask for the grace of shame and confusion [48]. A sense of sin, non-response, or negative response to such a loving God brings with it a very real sense of shame and confusion.

3. Give a setting that is real to what you are pondering. Set the stage in your imagination by asking God to take your imagination and use it for your prayer. Then begin to let your imagination give length and breadth to the prayer for you. When you are going to consider the sin of angels, this is hard because there is no material reality. But read the Scripture passages, and let your imagination give you some way of looking at the reality [47].

4. Then in the light of the Scripture, "prayerfully" consider the matter before you.

5. Go before Christ on the cross [53]. Here you will see the price of sin. Talk with him as he hangs on the cross. Talk to him as one friend talks to another; listen to him and respond to him as you find it natural to do. Ask him: How have I responded to you in the past (total, lived-out response, not just feeling)? How am I responding to you now? How should I respond to you? Let the prayer continue in this way for the hour. Then close the meditation with an Our Father.

6. After your prayer, during your time of reflection, make a note of anything that brought consolation during your prayer—feelings of peace, joy, union with God, or desolation—anxiety, discouragement, separation from God, agitation, avoidance. Ask yourself: Did I receive the grace I asked for, for example, shame and confusion because of sin? An understanding of sin from God's point of view? Jot down these things to be referred to at your next conference. (Cf. [77]).

Second Prayer Period

For the second prayer, which is about the sin of Adam and Eve, the director might suggest Gen. 2-3 from Scripture (Cf. [51]).

1. Use the same preparatory prayer as before.

   In fact, this will be consistent for every prayer period during the retreat.

2. The grace requested will be the same this time—an understanding of sin from God's point of view, with the accompanying response of a sense of shame and confusion. The grace one seeks will always fit the material to be prayed about.

3. The setting for this meditation is the Garden of Eden, with all its beauty.

4. Consider the matter prayerfully.

5. Before Christ on the cross, ask the same questions from the last meditation, entering into dialogue with him about whatever presents itself to mind. Close the prayer with an Our Father.

6. Do the reflection period: (a) consolations? (b) desolations? (c) Did I receive the grace I asked for? Jot these things down.

Third Prayer Period

The third prayer time is about the sin of one who chooses hell [52]. Some useful Scripture includes Rom. 1:18-2:11, Bar. 1:13-22, and 2 Tim. 3:1-9.

1. The preparatory prayer is the same.

2. Ask for the same grace.

3. The setting will be to imagine yourself as an exile, bound by sin.

4. Consider the matter carefully.

5. Go again before Christ on the cross and ask the same questions as before. Ignatius calls this dialogue with Christ a colloquy. There should always be a colloquy, a deliberate dialogue with Christ, or God, or some other about the matter considered in prayer. It should be done very naturally, however, expressing what one is feeling. The prayer is brought to closure with an Our Father.

6. Do the reflection, jotting down as before.

Fourth Prayer Period

The fourth prayer is a repetition of the first three periods [62]. Repetitions are very important to the Spiritual Exercise, and they do not prove redundant, as one might suspect.

1. Use the same preparatory prayer.

2. Ask for the same grace.

3. Use the setting as in the third period.

4. Consider prayerfully the consolations, the desolations, and the spiritual insights noted in the first three periods of prayer. If something brought consolation, savor it again, letting it deepen. If something brought desolation, return to it and let God confront you in whatever it is.

5. Ignatius suggests a triple colloquy for the repetitions [63-65]. Go first to Mary and talk with her, asking her to help you see the depth of your own sinfulness, the disorder of your actions flowing from this, and the spirit of the world that draws you to sinful action. Ask her to help you grow in the abhorrence of all this, that you may work against it. Sum it up with a Hail Mary.

Go to Jesus with the same petitions. Sum it up with Soul of Christ.

Then go to the Father, making the same request. Sum it up with an Our Father.

6. Do the reflection, jotting it down.

Fifth Prayer Period

The fifth exercise is a repetition of the fourth, using what was jotted down during the reflection times [64].

1. Use the same preparatory prayer.

2. Ask for the same grace.

3. Recall the setting.

4. Do the same kind of consideration of consolations, desolations, and insights.

5. Pray the triple colloquy.

6. Jot down reflections.

The difference between this and the preceding repetition is that by now the prayer should become simpler. Less thinking is needed, and that only in a summary way.

At this point, the director could explain the rest of the Additional Directions [73-90]. It is obvious that the fullest explanation is given for the first prayer period, with the director becoming more and more succinct in explaining each subsequent prayer period. Explanation is a tool meant to assure understanding on the part of the retreatant, but it should not be labored.

The Second Day

After praying about sin as it came into the world and as it has taken root and invades all of humankind, the retreatant, hopefully, will be experiencing a sort of oneness with all of sinful humanity. He or she can neither remain separate and aloof as though sin belongs only to others, nor turn inward and feel self-pity as the only one who sins. The director listens for an indication of either of these as well as for a sense of shame and confusion as the retreatant reports about the prayer of the previous day. The director then prepares the retreatant for a day of prayer on personal sin.

First Prayer Period

Because of sin's being diametrically opposed to one's right relationship with God, this day's first exercise might well be one of a call to holiness, as a way to put personal sin into perspective. Useful for this from Scripture are Eph. 1:3-14 and Ps. 139. The director assists the retreatant in seeing how to apply the structure to this meditation, using the format explained on the previous day:

1. Use the preparatory prayer.

2. Ask for the grace: to experience self as called to holiness, that is, to a life of response to a God who loves you personally.

3. As a setting recall the graces of the First Principle and Foundation.

4. Consider the matter prayerfully.

5. Colloquy with the God, asking God to keep you mindful of a great and personal love for you.

Close with an Our Father.

6. Jot down reflections.

Second Prayer Period

The second prayer will be from the text of the *Exercises* on personal sin [55-61]. This is not an examination of conscience as one would do for confession, but rather a recall of the development of sin in one's life.

1. Use the preparatory prayer.

2. Ask for the grace: a growing and intense sorrow and tears for your sins.

3. For the setting, picture yourself in a wasteland of disorder, like the Prodigal Son on the dung heap, alienated from God. Get a sense of exile.

4. Consider the text prayerfully.

5. Colloquy with Christ on the cross.

6. Jot down the reflections.

Third Prayer Period

Make a repetition, as in yesterday's fourth period.

Fourth Prayer Period

Make a repetition, as in yesterday's fifth period.

Fifth Prayer Period

The fifth exercise will be to consider hell [65-71]. Some persons find this exercise repelling. The director can help by suggesting that the retreatant, in setting the stage for the meditation, really consider what would be hell for this individual— being totally turned in on self forever, for example.

1. Use the preparatory prayer.

2. Ask for the grace: a growing and intense sorrow for sin, understanding it from God's point of view.

3. As the setting, imagine hell as it would be for you.

4. Open yourself to the matter and to the experience. There should not be much need for thinking. Rather, using all the senses, let yourself taste, smell, hear, see, and feel what it would be like to be thus for all eternity. (This approach introduces what Ignatius will later call "the application of the senses.")

5. In the colloquy, rejoice with God that hell need not be so for you. Talk with God about your experience and delight in God's saving love for you.

6. Jot down your reflections.

The Third Day

Although by now it is very probable that the retreatant is coming to know real sorrow for sin, still to come is the experience of the deep grace of knowing the love of God within that very sinfulness. The retreatant must remain with the subject matter until that grace is received. It is up to the director to keep suggesting Scripture texts that might facilitate the openness of the directee to that experience. The skillfulness of the director is sometimes most tested in this area.

First Prayer Period

Quite helpful can be prayer over Rev. 1-3. These letters to the churches often act as a stimulus to bid the retreatant toward a dialogue with God that opens him or her to the grace desired.

Second Prayer Period

The Prodigal Son/Daughter based in Luke 15:11-22 is sometimes done experientially, using as much time as is needed, and thus not establishing a certain number of prayer periods. It is done as follows:

1. Begin with a preparatory prayer.

2. Ask for the grace: as before, a growing and intense sorrow for sin.

3. Read the text and prepare to act out the story. Go to the chapel, or wherever you pray best. Ask God for your inheritance and write it all down; this will include your genetic inheritance, your talents, graces and so on. Then leave the chapel and the retreat house and go to another place in order to get the feeling of distance. There, mentally squander your whole inheritance, bit by bit, reviewing how it is that you do actually waste each part of it. When you have the feeling that it is all gone, and you have the experience of emptiness and absurdity, return to God in God's own house to finish the prayer. There, come before the loving God and let God receive you back with his unconditional love.

Third Prayer Period

If the Prodigal Son/Daughter does not take long, there may be a repetition. However, it often consumes the greater part of the retreatant's day. It often leads to a desire for the sacrament of reconciliation. When the director is not a confessor, there is still the distinct possibility that the retreatant will confess, in the full sense of the term, his or her sins to the director. In such cases the director extends forgiveness as one member of the Church to another. Celebration of that forgiveness within the actual sacrament remains to be experienced, even though the retreatant need not go into full detail again with the confessor to receive absolution. The special grace of feeling very loved within one's own sinfulness is sometimes only fully experienced in the celebration of the sacrament. The confession and full use of the sacrament of reconciliation do not necessarily occur at this time and should not be urged by the director. They should flow from grace.

The Fourth Day

Appropriate texts may continue to be used until the grace of the first week is evident. When this grace is experienced, it is usually good to give the retreatant an extra day for the deepening of the grace.

It is not long before the retreatant experiences either consolation or desolation during this First Week. The appropriate time for the director to explain what is happening is during this experience, by going over the Rules for Discernment of Spirits for the First Week [313-327]. Those for the Second Week [328-336] should not be explained until the retreatant experiences a need for them, after the First Week.

Chapter 4

The Kingdom of Christ

Dynamics of the Kingdom of Christ Meditation [91-99]

The meditation on the Kingdom of Christ is a concrete taking up again of the First Principle and Foundation [23], discovering its depth in the full light of Jesus Christ, so as to order one's life in the service of the Kingdom. Thus, the Kingdom meditation gives the thematic orientation to all the contemplations of the Second Week of the Spiritual Exercises.

I seek to discover Jesus Christ as a living person who focuses and unifies all my desires and gives ultimate meaning to my life through the call to me to give myself to him, along with the going out of myself that this gift requires of me. To work with Jesus Christ without seeking myself is to live the Kingdom. So, I contemplate the life of Jesus, always in view of this concrete desire. I want to give my life an orientation that will conform it to the pattern of Jesus in carrying out his mission from the Father.

Father Laplace points out that we do not make the Kingdom. It comes to us in Christ, the Word made flesh, and through the Church, his spouse [365]. So, we pray for the gift to be received into the Kingdom as co-workers with Jesus, not imagining this service a "generous role," like Peter imagined, but intensely praying for an open, waiting heart.

The risk of Christians, as of other people, is to live as if enclosed in the natural order, even though our inspiration and our vocabulary are Christian, and our concerns are apostolic. We confuse the success of the work we do with the achievement of the Kingdom. This can only lead to disappointment, as the Pharisees were disappointed in Jesus the Messiah. The Kingdom is not a human enterprise, but the life of the Divine Trinity filling the universe and all human beings incarnate in Jesus Christ, who continues his mission in ongoing history through his Church. Consequently, there is only one way to enter the Kingdom and to put ourselves at its service: the renouncing of self. This means not to make the Kingdom "my thing," but to give up my own ideas about how to achieve it—as Peter had to be led by Jesus to do—in order to work with him to achieve the Kingdom his way: through poverty, humiliations, and suffering.

To be at the service of the Kingdom, we must simply accept the unexpected of the person of Jesus Christ as he concretely presents himself to us through the Church today. A true turning around of the heart is necessary in order to give oneself to Jesus Christ as he is. It is a matter of losing one's life to save it, sacrificing oneself entirely through total self-giving. This is the paradoxical condition for the achievement of the Kingdom. Then Jesus can take me up entirely and use me according to God's will. I shall be a docile and willing instrument of the Holy Spirit, and the Kingdom will be made real through me.

The director will find it necessary to give to many retreatants exegetical and theological clarification of the Kingdom. In the Bible, the Kingdom is neither a people nor a place, but an event—the presence of the Holy One in our very midst in this world, in history, in people. This Kingdom has been won already through the death and resurrection of Jesus Christ. The Kingdom is within all human beings, the presence of the Spirit of the Risen Jesus. To preach the Kingdom is to bring people to recognize this presence of Christ in themselves, in all people, in the world. To achieve the Kingdom is to labor with Christ to bring all people to express their experience of the presence of Christ within them in their behavior—in the ways they relate to themselves, to other persons, to the world, and to God. This is why faith in the Kingdom cannot be separated from its behavioral expression in the life of individuals and of communities and in the organization of social, political, and economic structures, and in the way we treat the world (cf. Gen. 1:26-31; Rom. 8:19-22).

To work with Jesus Christ to bring the Kingdom to be is to strive to achieve social justice and true peace for all human beings, all living together in a community of love out of their communion in the shared experience of the presence of the Spirit of the Risen Jesus and manifesting in the community of all human beings together the life of Father, Son, and Holy Spirit. This is the meaning of the call of Christ the King: "It is my will to conquer the whole world and all my enemies, and thus to enter into the glory of my father" [95]. The glory of God is this incarnate manifestation of the inner life of the Trinity.

St. Paul perfectly describes the mission to bring the Kingdom to be:

> It is now my happiness to suffer for you. This is my way of helping to complete, in my poor human flesh, the full tale of Christ's afflictions still to be endured, for the sake of his body which is the Church. I became its servant by virtue of the task assigned to me by God for your benefit: to deliver his message in full; to announce the secret hidden for long ages and through many generations, but now disclosed to God's people, to whom it was His will to make it known—to make known how rich and glorious it is among all nations. The secret is this: Christ in you, the hope of a glory to come (Col. 1:24-27).

The impact of the Kingdom of Christ meditation will usually depend upon the director's ability to make its basic image, which is medieval, meaningful today. Experience shows that the results are worth the effort.[1]

Father Laplace notes that this is a parable, and it should be presented as one with its pivotal image being "a human king" [92-94]. Jesus often used a parable, with its image being something natural such as seeds, or personal such as the Prodigal Son, or historical, such as Jerusalem—all in order to help others to comprehend a spiritual dimension that cannot be grasped by reasoning. Thus, the true meaning of the visible is to mediate the invisible. The whole natural order of the universe is, in the biblical sense, an immense parable; that is, it is intended to speak to us of something else.

To serve the Kingdom, we must use all our natural talents and gifts; but we must not close these in upon themselves. This is the great risk: to close our human work in on itself, rather than always to see it as a parable of the Kingdom. The passage to the Kingdom of God is possible only through Jesus Christ.

In the concluding prayer of oblation, Ignatius expresses the foundation of all apostolic life [98]. The way to bring the Kingdom to be is the way of Jesus Christ: poverty, humiliations, pain. Thus, poverty is not an optional means to perfection; it is the *sine qua non* condition for achieving the Kingdom. The grace sought, then, is to realize and to relish that there can be nothing better than to be poor with Jesus, and that what is sought in laboring for the Kingdom is not just personal salvation but the salvation of the whole world.

The meditation on the Kingdom of Christ locates all the contemplations of the life of Jesus within the reality that faith in

---

1. Retreatants who are religious often find it very helpful in a repetition to hear the call articulated by the founder of their institute. The call is to labor for the Kingdom concretely according to the mission of the charism of the institute. One hears the founder pointing out what to eat, to drink, to wear, etc., in order to share in Christ's victory.

him cannot be separated from the struggle for social justice. Just as personal sin is inextricable from its social effect, so personal conversion is inextricable from social conversion (cf. [58:5], [106]). The call of Christ "to conquer the whole world" is a call to bring all human persons to express in their structured relationships with one another that "Christ is in you."

Proceeding With the Call of the King [91-99]

When the fruit of the First Week seems to have been received, it may be wise to ask the retreatant to give time for that grace to deepen. The rest of that same day should be sufficient for this. (Remember that a day goes from conference to conference.) The director can suggest that the retreatant unstructure the time and simply savor the grace received, or the time can be spent in formal prayer with Scripture texts that have come to hold special meaning. The desirable thing is simply to enjoy the day with God, rejoicing in God's love and praising God. This time precedes the meditation on the Call of the King, and it is not a "break day."

Some directors refer to the day that separates any two major sections of the Exercises as a "break day." Others call it a "day of repose." Whatever the words used, this day provides time for transition from one emphasis to another. It usually includes some relaxation from the intensity of the retreat.

This transition day into the Second Week seems to be the day that Ignatius intended for consideration of Christ our King. The "exercise should be gone through twice during the day" [99]. Relaxing after the First Week and preparing to enter the Second Week, the retreatant considers the material in one prayer period before taking the break and another at its conclusion.

In this chapter, I will offer two different ways in which a director may proceed with introducing this meditation to a retreatant.

One Method of Considering the Call of the King

1. Have a prayer period in the morning, using Psalm 95 as a good preparation for this.

2. Ask for the grace: "not to be deaf to his call" [91—Second Prelude]. The call to you now is the call to follow Christ our Lord. Although it may not yet be specific as to how, what is desired is to follow Christ wherever he leads, into the unknown without reserve, at whatever cost.

3. For the setting use Galilee and Judea, where Christ "reigned as king": in the market place among common, ordinary people like you and me, he was in this world, but not of this world.

4. Consider the parable [92-94]. This image of an earthly king comes out of the literature of Ignatius' time. In that period of history the relationship of the lord and his vassal was stronger than any other relationship. Entered into freely, it was sealed with a pledge symbolized by the clasping of both hands of the vassal within the hands of the lord. The relationship expressed therein designated a mutuality of the being protector, provider, leader, and friend.[2]

5. Look at the true King, Christ our Lord [95-97]. Apply to Jesus the same realities that are present in the parable. The relationship to which we are invited with him is even greater than the earthly relationship between king and vassal. Some Scripture passages that might be suggested are the following:

    Protector: Luke 22:31-32 "I have prayed for you . . ."
    John 10:1-18 Good Shepherd

---

2. "The Christ Experience and Relationship Fostered in the *Spiritual Exercises* of St. Ignatius of Loyola," *Studies in the Spirituality of Jesuits,* vol. VI, no. 5, October 1974, Robert L. Schmitt, S.J.

Provider:	Luke 11:11-13 "If you ask your father for a fish . . ."
	Luke 12:22-31 Providence of our God
Leader:	Matt: 5:6-7 Sermon on the Mount
	Matt: 16:24-28 Doctrine of the cross
Friend:	John 13-17 "I call you friends . . ."

6. Offer the prayer "Eternal Lord of all things . . ." [98]. At the close of the consideration of the Call of the King, a prayer is presented that is both a challenge and a call to the total following of the king; it is explicit in what it really means to follow Christ. Since the retreatant may not be able to say the prayer with utter sincerity immediately, the director listens carefully for growth in the retreatant's willingness to commit self to such a following. It is a good idea to ask the retreatant to write his or her own prayer using this one as a model, but only to do this at the end of the second consideration.

7. "Break Day" is spent in the "kingdom" that is the retreatant's own reality. It is spoken of as a "break day," but it is an integral part of the retreat. Therefore, the retreatant enjoys a day away from the retreat house. In the evening he or she might take about a half hour to reflect over the day and to see how it fits into the rest of the retreat, then get a good night's rest.

8. The morning of the next day should have one exercise before the conference, that is, a second consideration of the Call of the King.

Another Method of Considering the Call of the King

If I am going to follow somebody, I want the answer to four questions:

1. Who is this person in reality?

2. What is his or her cause?

3. What will it cost me? What will this person expect?

4. What will be the outcome I can expect?

It is sometimes helpful for a retreatant to consider these questions, applying them to Jesus. There are some Scripture passages that help. Not all these passages are necessary, but one or two can be helpful.

1. *Who is he, this Christ?*

Isa. 8:9-10   Terror for enemies
Isa. 9:1-17   Light, Child, Wonder-Counselor
Isa. 11:1-11   The great King
Isa. 12:6   "In our midst"
Isa. 42:1-4   First Servant Song
Isa. 49:1-7   Second Servant Song
Isa. 50:4-6   Third Servant Song
Isa. 52:13-53:12
Fourth Servant Song
Prologue of John's Gospel
"I am" passages:

John 6:35, 48, 51 Bread of Life; Living Bread
John 8:12   Light of the World
John 10:7,9   Gate of the Sheepfold
John 10:11,14   Good Shepherd
John 11:25   Resurrection
John 12:45   I, the light
John 14:15   The Way, the Truth and the Life
John 15:1, 5   The True Vine
John 14:9   Have I been with you all this time and still you do not know me?

2. *What is his cause?*

Matt. 5,6,7   Inaugural address

3. *What will he expect of me as a follower?*

Mic. 6:8   "Act justly, love tenderly, walk humbly" with him
Matt. 16:24-28 "If a person wishes to come after me . . ."
Luke 9:23-26 Conditions of discipleship
Zech. 8:16-23 "These are the things you must do . . ."

4. *What can I expect?*

Matt. 10:16-27 "They will cast you out of synagogues . . ."
Sir. 2   "Prepare yourself for an ordeal"
John 17:9-19   He will be with me.

The director might give all these passages if a person has a great deal of time to give to the Kingdom consideration, for instance if the conference time is later in the morning or in the afternoon. If all the passages are given, however, the retreatant should feel free to use any that are helpful but not necessarily all of them.

Chapter 5

The Second Week

Dynamics of the Second Week [101-189]

The goal of the Second Week, through contemplation of the human life of Jesus Christ, is to become open to the gradual transformation of my deep operational attitudes into his attitudes—the Beatitudes—so that I can discern truly how God calls me at all times to labor with Jesus to achieve the Kingdom; and to grow in passionate personal love of Jesus, so that I shall always follow him wherever he goes, even to Calvary and the cross [104]. Two texts of St. Paul beautifully sum up this goal:

> Now . . . you have discarded the old nature with its deeds and have put on the new nature, which is being constantly renewed in the image of its Creator and brought to know God (Col. 3:9).
>
> All of us, reflecting the splendor of the Lord in our unveiled faces, are being changed into likenesses to God, from one degree of splendor to another, for this comes from the Lord (Cor. 3:18).

First Contemplation [101-109]

In giving these contemplations, Ignatius always presents first the revealed Word of God to the retreatant through the history of the human life of Jesus given to us in the New Testament [102]. In the contemplation, I am to "draw profit from what I see" [106], from what I hear [107], and from what is done [108]. The movements experienced during prayer, then, are in response to the Word of God. Once again, the objective element always controls the subjective element.

Reference here is made for the first time to the Mysteries of the Life of Our Lord in numbers 261-312 of the *Exercises*: these provide Scripture texts and indications of focus in the continuing contemplation of the human life of Jesus.

Through means of three points, [106], [107], [108], Ignatius presents in this First Contemplation a tremendous panorama of salvation history, as revealed to us by God. He calls us to contemplate the situation of all peoples on the planet, individually and within their social structures, expressed in war [106], in their way of communicating with one another [107], and in wounding and killing one another [108]. The director can help the retreatant come to a consciousness of social sin and also of the inextricable relationship that exists between following Jesus out of faith that he is God, and laboring with him to bring the Kingdom to be in social justice and in peace among nations.

Second Contemplation [110-117]

The third point places the focus on the dynamic movement of Jesus' *way* of saving humanity—the first paces on the road to the cross. The retreatant is to "reflect and draw some spiritual fruit," that is, to keep seeking one's own place and own mission in the mystery of salvation still going on [116].

At this part of the retreat, the director gives attention to the change indicated for the Additional Directions [130, Note IV]. The total environment is an important help in preparing the retreatant to receive the grace being prayed for (*id quod volo*).

Introduction to the Consideration of Different States of Life [135]

Ignatius here indicates how to order the contemplations of the Second Week to help a person who is seeking to discern one's specific Christian vocation. In a retreat of personal renewal, the focus would rather be upon insights and movements experienced during these contemplations leading a person toward more authentic living of a vocation already discerned.

The Two Standards [136-148]

The third prelude leads the retreatant "to ask for what I desire" [139]. The grace sought is lucidity and spiritual intelligence, in order to be able to discern authentically how one is called to labor with Christ here and now to bring the Kingdom to be. This meditation makes explicit the value system of Jesus, already being revealed in the meditation on the Kingdom of Christ and in the previous contemplations of the Second Week. This gives the framework for all the succeeding contemplations—the norms of discernment seen in the life of Jesus himself.[1]

1. *First Part: The Standard of Satan* [140-142]. This is a parable of the Satanic dynamic—the active movement of darkness in the world: evil reaching everywhere, seeking to turn everyone away from God, from love, from the Kingdom and leading all to hell. The social dimension of evil, inextricable from personal sin, is again clear.

   The Satanic dynamic aims at destroying freedom and the ruling desire always to choose God, by disordering the *will to possess*, the *will to be esteemed*, and the will to be. Such disorder will lead to the spread of the dynamic of darkness in myself and, through me, in the world, like contagion.

2. *Second Part: The Standard of Christ* [143-147]. The points recall the specific grace of the meditation on the Kingdom of Christ: the *sine qua non* condition for following Christ and

---

1. See my "Ignatian Attitudes for Discernment," *Communal Discernment: New Trends*, SUBSIDIA AD DISCERNENDUM 14 (Rome: Centrum Ignatianum Spiritualitatis, 1975), pp. 35-44.

laboring with him to bring the Kingdom to be is total spiritual poverty, always affective, and also effective if God so calls me; the true indifference and the ruling desire only to go to God, whatever other loves must be relinquished (cf. [23]).

Serving as the seed of the Third Kind of Humility [167], the three steps that place one under the Standard of Christ can be articulated as: (1) wholly open spiritual freedom, "poverty"; (2) and total vulnerability, "insults and contempt"; (3) which enable one unconditionally to love God and other people, "humility."

Three Classes of Persons [149-157]

In the mental representation of the second prelude, a person with an apostolic vocation can well include "all human persons whom I am called to serve with Christ" [151]. The grace sought in the third prelude is the determination to act out of spiritual lucidity, to live out the choices reached through authentic discernment [152].

As to the further note [157], Father Laplace remarks that the effort here is to react vigorously against hidden resistance to the call of the Lord. I pray for the grace to be able to make my interior, affective detachment so real that I can make it effective, if God calls me to do so. I am seeking transcendence from environmental supports, insofar as there may be an inordinate dependence on these, and to experience full awareness of my absolute dependence on God alone, enabling me freely to make choices for God's service and to act upon them.

Three Kinds of Humility [165-168]

Ignatius suggests that during the time of the election—the effort to discern the call of God to me during this retreat—the retreatant often should repeat the colloquy of the Two Standards [147], while making the various contemplations [159]. This particular colloquy by now should be a summing up of the continuity of insights and of movements experienced in the previous exercises, all directed toward being received totally under the Standard of Christ: "I just want to be with you."

To establish the interior climate for these exercises of election, Ignatius proposes that we consider the Three kinds of humility—"in order that we may be filled with love of the true doctrine of Christ" [164], that is, in order that our ruling desire may be to follow Christ in his way of serving God and of saving humanity.

These three kinds of humility are three degrees of centering oneself more and more in God, rather than in self. In the *Autograph Directory*, Ignatius refers to these as three degrees of indifference.[2] They may also be called three degrees of love, because they describe three degrees of self-giving to Jesus. Nothing new is added here, really, to the oblation of the Kingdom of Christ meditation or to the commitment of oneself to labor under the Standard of Christ; but, through this consideration, one seeks to deepen within his or her entire conscious and affective being the consequence of this total oblation and this commitment—total surrender of self to Jesus Christ always, following him wherever he goes.

1. *The First Kind of Humility* [165]. Here is a person whose spiritual freedom is such that inordinate desires would never lead one for any reason whatsoever to exclude God from his or her life in a centering of self totally upon oneself.

2. *The Second Kind of Humility* [166]. This corresponds to the perfect indifference of the Principle and Foundation [23]. It is a spiritual freedom that enables one to desire only the service of God, so that the source of all choices is solely the love of God. This is the love described by Ignatius at the beginning of the Second Way of Making a Choice of a Way

---

2. *Directoria Exercitiorum Spiritualium, 1540-1599* (Rome: Historical Institute of the Society of Jesus, 1955), #17, pp. 74-77.

of Life during the third time of election, the love at the very source of all authentic Christian choices: that the "love that moves and causes one to choose must descend from above, that is, from the love of God, so that . . . one chooses . . . solely because of one's Creator and Lord" [184]. This is the basic existential attitude of total surrender to the concrete call of God at all times.

3. *The Third Kind of Humility* [167]. This moves to a different level of personal love for Jesus Christ. God was so carried away by love that the second person of the trinity became human to be delivered over to people, in order to suffer and die and in this way to redeem the world. In the pierced Heart of Jesus we see the embodiment of God's love for us.

The third kind of humility is the language of a person who knows what it is to "fall in love." The only reason for choosing the third kind of humility is to be with the beloved, literally and locally in the experience where the Beloved most visibly and undeniably expressed the depth of God's love for us. "So Christ was treated before me." Because of personal love for Jesus, a person wants to follow him wherever he goes, actually to be more like him by choosing his way of love: the way of the cross.

This is simply the natural psychology of any great personal love: the need to be with the beloved, to share his or her life, to suffer what he or she suffers. One can surely verify this from one's own experience of human love, which encompasses the desire to suffer with someone beloved who is in pain or grief. A person's passionate personal love of Jesus establishes a basic, existential attitude driving one to be united with him in his suffering love. The third kind of humility makes sense only as the intrinsic dynamic of passionate personal love, which demands an utterly gratuitous act as the only adequate way to express such love. Love is the *only* reason. There is no other.

The interior attitude of the third kind of humility passes naturally into acts, and one will have a bias to choose poverty and humiliations and the cross, if these choices would not diminish God's glory or lessen one's apostolic service. This is what Ignatius means by saying that these choices suppose the "equal praise" of God; all of one's choices are for "greater . . . service to the Divine Majesty" [168]. However, when this service leads one with Christ through poverty and humiliations to the cross, the person having the third kind of humility will experience joy in the deepest self because the basic thrust of his or her spirit is to be *with* Jesus.

The Election [169-189]

The "election" of the *Spiritual Exercises* as presented by Ignatius concerns the choice of one's Christian life-vocation. Ignatius notes Three Times When a Correct and Good Choice of a Way of Life May Be Made [175-177].

The first two times are made through the discernment of spirits [328-336]. Both of these times of election terminate in the confirming experience of the unique, gifted peace that is the witness of the Holy Spirit, the testimony of God, within one's own spirit (1 John 5;7-10). The only difference between the First Time of election [175] and the Second Time [176] is that of duration. In the First Time, confirmation of the election is experienced immediately, as soon as one sees the evidence—which it may previously have taken a long time to gather and to clarify—through which God speaks God's actual word to one here and now. In the Second Time, it takes a longer or shorter period of testing the spirits (1 John 4:1), by one's following the orientation of movements of consolation and of desolation, finally to arrive at the experience of confirmation.[3] During this dis-

---

3. For a development of election by discernment of spirits and of the experience of confirmation, see my "Ignatian Discernment," *Studies in the Spirituality of Jesuits*, vol. II, no. 2 (April, 1970), and also, "The Still, Small Voice," *The Way*, vol. II, no. 4, (October, 1971) pp. 275-282. See "Discernment of Spirits II," in Part III.

cernment of spirits, whether or not it takes place within a retreat, the help of a good spiritual director is most important to assist the directee to objectify his or her spiritual experiences and to aid the person to be truly interiorly free.

The confirmation experience, terminating the period of one's discerning the movements of consolation and desolation, verifies that the retreatant found *God* moving him or her to this election. It is God who determines the election to be made: "Whatever state or way of life God our Lord may grant us to choose" [135]. This is already clear in the colloquies of the meditation on the Kingdom of Christ [91-98] and on the Two Standards [136-147], when the exercitant offers self for a life of actual poverty," "should Thy most holy majesty deign to choose and admit me to such a state and way of life" [98]; and, "should the Divine Majesty be pleased thereby, and deign to choose and accept me" [147]. Similarly, those in the Third Class of Persons wish to keep their money or not, only "as God our Lord inspires them" [155]. In the *Autograph Directory*, Ignatius remarks that through the experience of consolations and desolations, the retreatant will discern to which choice God moves one.[4]

The Third Time of election [177] is called for when there is need to come to a decision within a definite time, and the experience of confirmation is not given within that period of time. Movements of the Holy Spirit can be experienced only if the Spirit gives them, and one cannot put the Holy Spirit on a timetable. Hence, Ignatius says that this Third Time is a "time of tranquility, that is, a time when the soul is not agitated by different spirits, and has free and peaceful use of its natural powers." Movements are not being experienced by the person, and also one is not in desolation, when no decision should be made [318]. Thus, the Lord is calling the person to make this election out of prayerful reflection, Christian prudence, and the

---

4. *Directoria Exercitiorum Spiritualium, 1540-1599* (Rome: Historical Institute of the Society of Jesus, 1955), #18, p. 76.

help of the director. This time of election is a concrete application of the Principle and Foundation [23] to one's life. Ignatius provides some very effective means to ensure that a person has the interior freedom necessary to make a good election in the Third Time [178-188].[5]

Father Laplace has provided some helpful questions to aid in one's making the Third Time of election of a state of life. The response to these questions should be made in prayer and peace. If the person is not in "tranquility," but is feeling disturbed, the election should be postponed. Nothing good can be done in fear and agitation.

1. Do you feel that you have enough maturity, as a person and as a Christian, to make a decision in complete freedom? What reasons might make you doubtful about this maturity?

2. What graces do you think you have received from God since your childhood? It would be well to make a kind of global review of the history of God in your life.

3. Concretely, since you have been old enough to understand and to will, what have you wanted to do with your life?

4. In the light of the retreat, how do you judge this desire?

5. If this desire seems to you to conform to the ideal of the Gospel, what obstacles seem to oppose its realization? State obstacles that arise from other people, from circumstances of life and, in particular, from yourself—childhood or youth, education, temperament, faults, and so on.

---

5. An excellent concrete application of this Third Time of election is provided by Ignatius in the Rules for the Distribution of Alms [337-344]. The director will find these rules useful for helping the retreatant in many ways, applying their principles to the specific concerns of that person. For instance, these principles can aid in ordering toward God relationships with people through affection or ministry, so that all the love that moves one is "from above, that is, from the love of God our Lord" [338]. These principles can also help the director reflecting upon his or her own feelings toward the directee.

6. In the past, has this desire given you joy and peace? In what circumstances? And now, in the light of the love of Christ, what effect does this desire have on you?

7. Is there, in your estimation, a special motive that seems to incline you in one direction rather than another? Before God, how do you judge this motive?

8. How do persons who know you well—for example, parents, friends, priest, counselors—react to your desire?

9. What effect does the thought of rejection of this desire produce in you?

It would be well, as a help to oneself, to answer these questions in writing, doing so as simply as possible and dropping out any questions to which there seems to be no answer.

When the choice of a state of life has already been made, the retreat election concerns one's becoming aware of the call of the Lord here and how to fulfill this Christian vocation and to respond totally to its call—what Ignatius calls the Amendment and Reformation of One's Way of Living in One's State of Life [189]. The election of a personal renewal retreat differs from mere resolutions, which are aimed at the necessary self-discipline required to live as true Christians. The elements of such discipline and of concomitant resolutions do not require deep discernment. They usually leap to the eye, at least of other persons, if not of oneself.

The election of the Spiritual Exercises is operative on a much deeper level. It concerns the orientation of my inner being, the basic, existential attitude that governs my whole life-style, the fundamental notion, rich and deep, around which all else is organized and which will unify my life and simplify it more and more. The discovery of this orientation supposes a long, interior preparation—that of the Spiritual Exercises—which reveals the deep obstacles within me to true spiritual freedom, all in order that I can give myself completely to labor with Christ to bring the Kingdom to be.

The election, then, is not something dramatic or dreamlike. Having discovered during the retreat the particular form of self-love that limits my actual living out my total commitment to Christ, I shall feel the need to concentrate precisely on this. This will polarize my efforts in the future and be the living out of the interior liberation experienced through making the Exercises.

What I seek, therefore, is a summing up of the gifts of God to me as best as I can now see them, bringing to focus the work of the Holy Spirit in me during these Exercises. Further experiences of the Spiritual Exercises in the future will move in the same direction, making this orientation and all of its implications more and more precise. It is not so much a matter of searching as it is of discovering what the Lord has worked in me.

Ignatian Contemplation

"In Christ the whole plenitude of God is embodied and dwells in him, and it is in him that you find your completion" (Col. 2:10).

In order to enter into the life of God, eternally existing as Blessed Trinity, we must enter into the concrete, historical life of Jesus as it is present to us *now*. In contemplating the words and actions of Jesus of Nazareth, who lived two thousand years ago, we must act in the fullness of faith in the mystery of the Word made flesh. The humanity of God in the words and actions of Jesus Christ is present for every person throughout continuing salvation history, because they are the words and actions of a person existing eternally. What he once said and did has now become eternity, and Jesus Christ still approaches us through these events. The mysteries that he lived in his flesh preserve their efficaciousness and in some way their reality in Jesus risen and glorified, the existing Christ whom we meet in all our contemplations. Ignatius, then, is not asking for an effort of imaginary presence alone, but for awareness of a spiritual reality: the mystery still living in Christ.

I must pray for faith in the truth of this mystery and know that I meet him in contemplating his human life in the Gospel. Without this kind of prayer, I can never achieve the basic, existential attitude of openness to the word of God, which comes to me here and now in every concrete situation. Personal contemplation of the human life of Jesus is the essential means to accomplish the vivification of faith that enables me truly to hear and discern the word of God at all times and really to encounter Christ in other people, in my work and in the world.

Karl Rahner has pointed out very well:

> Only a constant relationship to the "historical" Jesus, only a repeated meditation on the mysteries of his life, and only an increasing listening to his word can produce the kind of imitation of Christ that knows what it is doing and so grow to fruition. We must not forget that our reflective knowledge is not just reflective, but that it has a formative influence on what takes place in the depths of the soul. If this is the case, then we must *consciously* follow Christ; then we must knowingly pattern our lives after the life of the "historical" Jesus of Nazareth.[6]

The great petition that Ignatius insists that the retreatant repeat in all contemplations of Jesus during the Second Week, no matter what mystery is being considered, is to ask for an *interior knowledge* of Jesus, our Lord, in order to *love* him more deeply and to follow him more closely [104]. This requires gathering together all of one's most profound powers—to have an interior knowledge, to encounter the living Christ, through an intimate, personal experience of him. It is to know him not as one might imagine him, but as he truly is, a knowledge not just of his ac-

---

6. Karl Rahner, S.J., *Spiritual Exercises*, trans. Kenneth Baker, S.J., (New York: Herder and Herder, 1965), p. 117.

tions and feelings but of his very being. It is knowledge not of the humility of Jesus, but of Jesus humble. This interior knowledge is the condition of truly effective love, love that united an individual to the *living* Jesus. Such love is the source of true service, service not of an ideal, but of a living person. This service consists precisely in becoming another Christ at all times, becoming another humanity for Jesus in one's own unique way.

In contemplating the mysteries of Christ's life, I must see, feel, relish all that he is, realizing that he actually lives, finding in him—and not in some kind of heady analysis—his goodness, his love, his self-giving, his holiness. I must allow the inner dynamism of his life to be operative in my life in my own personal situations, so that I can embody the Word of God here and now.

In the contemplations of the mysteries of the life of Jesus, Ignatius gives a "history" as well as an imaginative representation of the scenes, persons, and actions [102]. The history inserts us into the objective revelation of the Word of God, whereas the imaginative representation is a way, much like a movie, to help us compose our whole being and to open ourselves to the action of the Holy Spirit mediated by the Word. This is necessary, because Jesus entered the world of space and time; and we ourselves exist multidimensionally as body-persons. But it is, nevertheless, merely a means. We should neither attach ourselves to it too much, nor abandon it under a pretext of "pure prayer." We should see the imaginative representation, rather, as a sign that points beyond itself to a personal encounter with the Lord. We must not be so wedded to the bodily and temporal appearance that we cannot discern in it Jesus Christ.

Just as in the celebration of the liturgy, we must not attach ourselves so much to the liturgical event as to the mystery that it signifies, so the same is true for the imaginative representation in contemplation of the mysteries of the life of Jesus. The contemplation must be the exercise of our faith. We are in the presence of Jesus in his mysteries in the measure that we exercise our faith. We must pray to realize that this presence of faith is more real than the presence of beings to one another in the human order. It is faith that introduces us into the heart of reality.

These exercises are contemplations, not theological analyses. The Bible is very anthropomorphic. The People of God wished to have some understanding of their relationship with God, and so they pictured God in terms of human personality in space and time. When Ignatius imagines the Trinity looking upon the world and deciding to save it, he is very biblical [102]—he is not speculating in some metaphysical framework upon the eternity of the Unmoved Mover. The director should help each retreatant making these contemplations to follow the lead of one's own temperament, imagination, and feelings, thus seeking signs that will lead one in faith to personal, transforming encounter with Jesus Christ. The time of the Spiritual Exercises is a privileged time for discovering one's own best method of prayer here and now, perhaps radically revising the method from what it has been up to now.

In his presentation of the contemplation of the Nativity, Ignatius illustrates his method, very simple, very rich in homey details [110-117]. His purpose is that we shall slowly, gently enter into the spirit of Jesus Christ and come to know him more intimately, love him more deeply, follow him more closely. One is to look *long* at Jesus in the light of one's own concrete call to share in his mission to save all humanity and to transform the world. Throughout all the contemplations, Ignatius focuses our attention sharply on Jesus' way of saving—the way of the cross.

Rather than bringing the Gospel down to one's own level, one must open oneself to be lifted by the Holy Spirit to the level of the Gospel. Once again, the objective element always controls the subjective element. One must trust in faith that this contemplation of the Gospel is a seed, a sowing in faith that grows by its own dynamic spiritual power.[7]

Ignatius calls the retreatant to *look long* at Jesus—his words, his actions, his interior attitudes, his confrontations, his way of carrying out his mission. One must look long: rest in the mystery, let it penetrate to the depths of the heart. The prayer opens one to the Holy Spirit, realizing the wonder chanted by St. John in the beginning of his First Letter:

> It was there from the beginning; we have heard it; we have seen it with our own eyes; we looked upon it and felt it with our own hands; and it is of this we tell (1 John 1:1).

It is this looking long that will bring a person to an interior knowledge and relish that transforms one in Christ. The director should help the retreatant to avoid seeking applications in life too quickly or trying to see everything at once. The light of the Holy Spirit comes as gradual enlightenment. One should draw everything possible from the present contemplation, making felt movements of both consolation and desolation pass to the level of faith. These movements should be noted as *facts* in order to see later whether the Spirit takes them up again.[8] Such contemplation is a real purification of imagination and of understanding, passing over entirely to the level of faith through the intense looking long at the mysteries of Jesus Christ.

Ignatian contemplation, then, is not a little imaginary play, but *presence in faith* to a past event in order to let the Word of God penetrate us and transform us. This is why one must look long. Much time is necessary to move to such a level of faith. The division of the contemplations into three points is Ignatius' ingenious way to help the retreatant to rest for a long time in

---

7. For an excellent and comprehensive scriptural and theological treatment of Ignatian contemplation, see David M. Stanley, S.J., "Contemplation of the Gospels, Ignatius Loyola and the Contemporary Christian," *Theological Studies*, vol. XXIX (September, 1968) pp. 417-443.

8. See the first two chapters in Part III.

contemplating the same mystery, to look long and to allow the mystery slowly to penetrate one's spirit. Thus, he directs the retreatant to return three times to the identical scene, first, seeing the different persons [106]; then listening to what they say [107]; and, finally, considering what they do [108].

1. *Seeing the persons*: Note the richness of detail Ignatius gives as a model for the retreatant to develop his or her own richly detailed, concrete image. What he calls for is that the retreatant look long at each person, like letting oneself deeply appreciate the details in a painting, and allowing the Holy Spirit to give the interior movements that can come to one who "draws profit from what I see."

2. *Listen to what they say*: Again Ignatius invites attention to rich detail, having the retreatant listen to the words supplied by Scripture or by imagination, and once again allow the Holy Spirit to give the interior movements, as well as the insights that can come to one who "draws profit" from what I hear.

3. *Considering what they do*: By looking long at the actions of the persons seen in rich detail, the retreatant again allows the Holy Spirit to give the interior movements and also the insights that can come to one who "draws some fruit from each of these details."

The threefold contemplation of the same mystery from these different points of view is a powerful aid to the retreatant in learning to look long and also to notice one's own pattern of movements of consolation and desolation and also of deepening insights.

Ignatius supposes that throughout the period of contemplation, one will follow the movements of the Spirit, including speaking to the persons in colloquies. Nevertheless, he insists that each exercise "should be closed with a colloquy" [109]. In the dynamic of Ignatian contemplation, this closing colloquy has the vital function of focusing the grace received (*id quod volo*) according to the personal movements of the Spirit experienced by each retreatant. "According to the light that I have received, I will beg for grace to follow and imitate more closely our Lord" [109].

Thus, Ignatius stands back. He does not tell the retreatant what to obtain from the contemplations, other than in general: deeper knowledge of Jesus Christ, in order to love him more intensely and to follow him more closely. He avoids telling the retreatant how the response to Jesus should be realized in the concrete. He simply presents the mystery to be contemplated and leaves it to the Holy Spirit to move the retreatant as the Spirit will. The closing colloquy, then, is a personal summing up in prayer of the movements of the entire contemplation experienced by the retreatant.

This is especially clear when Ignatius calls for a Threefold Colloquy. After one has made the meditation on the Two Standards [136-148], Ignatius prescribes a triple colloquy for the close of every succeeding contemplation [159]. Following the movements experienced during each contemplation, the retreatant is to ask for the grace to be received under the Standard of Christ. Thus, the meditation on the Two Standards functions as the framework of all the contemplations, providing the basis for true spiritual discernment. Through the closing colloquy, too, the retreatant prays, if necessary, for the total effective detachment described in the Note after the Three Classes of Persons [157].

The closing colloquies of the continuing contemplations enable the retreatant more and more to clarify and to follow the orientation of the movements of the Holy Spirit, and to prepare the way for discernment of the call of the Lord that will be the election. Furthermore, the closing colloquies facilitate the progressive simplification of prayer toward the "application of the senses" [121-126].

Prayer Periods: Number and Kind

The dynamic movement of the prayer periods is established the first day of the Second Week: two contemplations, followed by two repetitions of movements and insights, leading to the application of the senses. It is a dynamic of entering more and more deeply into the movements of the Holy Spirit within this individual retreatant and, so, of more and more simplification of a prayer that gradually becomes passive under the movements of the Spirit. Ignatius indicates that "to attain better what is desired," it might help to make only four prayer periods a day "from the second day to the fourth inclusive" [133]. He seems to contradict himself by prescribing five periods on the fourth day, the day of the Two Standards [148]. On the second and third days, he still proposes contemplation of two mysteries, a repetition, and the application of the senses [133].

From the fifth day on, Ignatius returns to five prayer periods a day. However, he now proposes only one mystery a day for contemplation; but he says to contemplate it twice, then to make two repetitions and the application of the senses [159]. Ignatius supposes that, through the dynamic of contemplative prayer initiated the first day of the Second Week, the retreatant now will be able to experience more movements and to draw more profit from less material for contemplation, through the increasing simplification of prayer and the deepening experience of the grace of the Second Week (*id quod volo*).

The repetitions are a crucial element in the dynamic of Ignatian contemplation. These do not mean to review everything that went on during a period of contemplation of a mystery. Rather, "we should pay attention to and dwell upon those points in which we have experienced greater consolation or desolation or greater spiritual appreciation" [62]. Again, "attention should always be given to some more important parts in which one has experienced understanding, consolation, or desolation" [118]. This is how, during a day of retreat, one little by little comes to progressive simplification of prayer and increasing clarity about the orientation of the movements of the Holy Spirit within one. The experience during prayer becomes less that of ideas and images and more that of a *Presence* drawing us by more and more simple means.

Through the dynamic of the repetitions one moves toward "applying the five senses to the matter of the . . . contemplations" at the end of the day [121]. Within an age-old tradition of Christian praying rooted in Scripture: "Taste and see that the Lord is sweet" (Ps. 34:9), Ignatius uses the external senses as a parable of interior, passive experience of the Lord, since what characterizes the senses is precisely passive experience of the realities received or undergone. Thus, building upon the increasing simplification of prayer through the preceding contemplations and repetitions and upon the focusing of movements through the closing colloquies, Ignatius offers a way of prayer intended to open the retreatant to passive, infused contemplation, if the Holy Spirit grants it.

Out of his own prayer experience, Ignatius supposes that, after the successive contemplations and repetitions, the entry into the scene through each of the five senses will open one to receive the movements of the Holy Spirit at a much deeper level of the heart—the center of interiority. Such simplification of prayer requires intense recollection during the day and a special grace of God. We can only dispose ourselves. God gives when God will the relish for the infinite sweetness of the divinity; but one instant of this is worth all the labor of disposing oneself.

The director should help the retreatant to enter into the application of the senses. The method consists in making oneself present to the mystery at the deepest level through interior sight, hearing, touch—all the "spiritual" senses. Here, as always, different people have different aptitudes and attractions. Some persons are led to interior passivity more through seeing, others through hearing, or another sense, according to the suggestions of Ignatius [122-125]. Some persons focus on detail, while others approach the mystery globally. The great secret is always to make oneself interiorly present to the scene—an opening of one's consciousness into the scene, going right into it and being there simply as an awareness of what is going on. One allows the scene, the words, the actions, the persons contemplated to produce their own effects in the depths of one's heart. Depending upon circumstances, the retreatant will exercise more or less personal activity during each prayer; but one, finally, must always allow the mystery of Christ to reach to the depths of one's heart to transform it.

All of the above may be more readily understood if I provide one example of a particular mystery to show how it serves as the basis for prayer during four or five periods on a typical day of the retreat.

The director may have his or her retreatants contemplate The Life of Christ our Lord from the Age of Twelve to the Age of Thirty [271]. One person may be drawn to dwell especially on the humble, human virtues of Jesus, truly a child and truly a man, and his submission to the law of human labor, and, so, be given insights about these dimension's of one's own life. Another may be moved during the initial prayer period into looking long at Jesus' response to God and to the people around him during his years of growing up and of young manhood, and then experience insights and movements from the Holy Spirit about one's own responses to God and to people in one's own routine, daily life. Or some person experiencing a time of formation or growth may be focused especially on following Jesus moving through his own steps of growth and of preparation for his mission and draw profit from this. Someone having problems with authority and obedience may be drawn into the mystery of the obedience of Jesus to human authority and be given needed lights and movements from contemplating this. A person struggling to become "as a little child" may be given insights into the openness of Jesus as a child. In the one or two contemplations of the mystery, the Holy Spirit will move each retreatant according to the needs of each person now, and this mystery can be a source of rich and deep interior understanding and relish over a long period of time, even though the mystery is revealed in only two verses of Scripture (Luke 2:51-52).

For repetitions, the retreatant should come back to contemplation of seeing persons or hearing words or watching actions that were the source of special insights or movements of consolation or desolation. Through the repetitions, normally a deepening of these insights and movements and a simplifying of the act of contemplation will be experienced.

The application of the senses, then, will flow into more and more passivity through the previous progression of ever greater deepening and simplification. Thus, going back to scenes where insights and movements have become increasingly profound, the retreatant is invited by Ignatius, "with the aid of the imagination to apply the five senses to the subject matter" [121]. And so, according to the pattern of lights and movements already given, the retreatant selects from among the rich details of this mystery what suits this individual and enters into the application of the senses. For example:

1. *First Point.* "Seeing in imagination . . . contemplating and meditating in detail the circumstances in which they are" [122].

> SEE - the details of family life at Nazareth;
> - how Jesus, Mary, and Joseph look at different times, as Jesus grows up and as they grow older: their faces, bodies, hands, nonverbals;
> - how their home is furnished by Joseph's carpentry and Mary's interior decoration and little things that Jesus makes;
> - the clothing that Mary makes for them;
> - their vegetable garden and flowers and trees;
> - the town and the neighbors and the scenery;

WATCH - Mary cooking, going to market, carrying the jug to the town well, bringing a cool drink to Joseph in the shop;
- Joseph working and teaching Jesus carpentry;
- Jesus playing games;
- Jesus studying the Scriptures:
- Jesus being obedient to Mary and Joseph and growing in wisdom and age and grace.

2. *Second Point.* "To hear what they are saying, or what they might have to say" [123].

LISTEN TO - their family conversation, their family prayers, their family silences;
- Mary talking with her woman friends at the town well;
- Joseph arranging carpentry business;
- Jesus swapping stories with his playmates;
- the mourning of Jesus and Mary when Joseph dies.

3. *Third Point.* "To smell the infinite fragrance and taste the infinite sweetness of the divinity. Likewise to apply these senses to the soul and its virtues, and to all according to the person we are contemplating" [124].

SMELL - laundry hanging out to dry;
- fresh cut wood and the sweat of hard work;
- the fragrance of their virtues.

TASTE - the food they eat, the bread that is broken;
- the wine they drink, the cup that is shared;
- the air they breathe;
- the sweetness of their love of God and of one another.

4. *Fourth Point.* "To apply the sense of touch, for example, by embracing and kissing the place where the persons stand or are seated" [125].

> FEEL - the texture of their clothing;
> - the shape of their furniture and the grain of the wood;
> - warmth in summer and cold in winter;
> - the atmosphere of peace and love.

Through the aid of the imagination to apply the five senses, Ignatius provides a method for the retreatant to open oneself to experience passive transformation by the Holy Spirit into more and more knowing, loving and following Jesus in one's own life.

Reflection on Prayer

A practical help to the retreatant for identifying the insights and movements for repetitions leading to the application of the senses is Ignatius' fifth Additional Direction: "After an exercise is finished, either sitting or walking, I will consider for the space of a quarter of an hour how I succeeded in the meditation or contemplation" [77]. The focus of this Additional Direction is upon the retreatant's own efforts and fidelity to the exigencies of prayer. However, it also provides the opportunity immediately after a prayer period to reflect upon and refine the insights and the orientation of movements synthesized during the closing colloquy. These become the matter for prayer during the repetitions, as well as for sharing with the director during the conference. It is good to suggest to the retreatant, as Ignatius seems to do, that a specific change of bodily position will be helpful here to initiate those minutes. One clearly can distinguish the time of prayer from the time of reflection on prayer and not fall into the temptation to watch oneself praying while praying.

The director must help the retreatant to overcome the common tendency to judge the "success" of prayer according to one's own idea of it: consolations, no distractions, *myself* praying well. The true good of prayer is the formation of the basic, existential attitude of total surrender to the Lord at all times. God alone can give this good through the more or less active cooperation of one's efforts. Ignatius would have a person return during a repetition to movements of desolation as well as of consolation; a maxim of good directors is, "when in desolation, stay there." Sometimes God can give light only by leading one through darkness. At times during prayer, a person may experience being lost in one's own incapacity, weighed down with aridity and distractions, and that one's presence to God, like a flickering fire, simply must be constantly renewed with a few prayerful words or a felt attitude. Yet, through such prayer, one can become aware of the gift of an interior relish, sometimes hardly felt or apparently smothered under a whirl of selfish feelings or wild distractions or even vivid repugnance. But this interior relish finally becomes a power, actually a gifted strength to serve God with one's whole being, no matter what the cost, until death. Such is the pearl of great price which is always to be sought in prayer. This is what transforms a person into Christ and prepares one always to surrender to the call of the Lord here and now.

A Prayer During the Second Week

Lord, Jesus Christ,
   help me to discover you as a living
         person,
   who focuses and unifies all my desires
     and gives meaning to my life,
      through the total gift of myself to
        you
      and the going out of myself

that this gift demands.
Give me the grace to labor with you
without seeking myself—
to live the Kingdom
in its full reality.

Moving Into the Second Week [100-189]

The Second Week of the Spiritual Exercises brings one into a contemplation of the earthly life of Jesus. Therefore, the prayer begins to have a setting of time and place as it was experienced by him. So, after the usual preparatory prayer asking that "all . . . be directed purely to his praise and service" [46], [101], the retreatant recalls the history, or time dimension, of the mystery to be contemplated; then he or she establishes a place, or space dimension with memory and imagination.

An important difference between meditation and contemplation should be explained here. In meditation one thinks about the matter prepared and talks with God about it, whereas in contemplation one enters into the mystery presented. This latter can be done actively, by conscious effort, as one uses imagination and memory to project self into the time and space of Jesus as he was relating with persons—seeing him, listening to him, entering into the scene and interacting with him. And it can also be done passively, by one's being drawn into the mystery by God, with a person discovering that one "is there" and thus losing all awareness of bodily locality and circumstances; only upon later reflection does one realize how intimately he or she has been into the mystery with Jesus. While not setting up false expectations, the director should instruct the retreatant in the art of active contemplation and leave it to God to draw the individual into a more passive intimacy as God so desires.

The grace asked for in each prayer period in this Second Week is that of "an intimate knowledge of our Lord, who has become a man for me, that I may love him more and follow him more closely" [104].

The First Day

First Exercise. Speaking naturally and often without the text, the director introduces the Incarnation [101-109] and the method of contemplating it, using words similar to the following:

1. Use the preparatory prayer as usual and then read the Scripture, Luke 1:26-38.

2. Since we have time [102] and place [103] to consider, let us start with the Trinity and their moment of decision about the need to express more clearly the loving God, whom the world seems to persist in not recognizing. Look with the Trinity upon the whole world: what do you see but the world in need of redemption and still, today, acting as if the redeeming act never took place. God is not yet incarnate in the decision rooms of transnational corporations, in the special interest groups that manipulate governing bodies of nations, in the cover-ups and intrigues that are so much a part of society.

   Listen to the Three Divine Persons come to the decision of the Incarnation, and even take a part in that decision if you are so drawn.

   Observe as the angel Gabriel goes to Nazareth to present Mary with the question on which hinges the divine plan. Are there still some individuals and groups of individuals who open themselves in an unconditional "yes" as Mary did? What are the implications of this? Be careful not to let yourself get sidetracked into idle daydreaming. Stay with the Lord and let him direct your attention.

3. See in imagination the whole world, letting your vision come to rest on the village of Nazareth and the house where

Mary lives. Give it real dimension and color as you see it. Accuracy as to the reality of that time does not matter; what does matter is that you can be there, too, to see, to hear, to observe, and to interact as everything takes place, doing so as you are drawn into the mystery that changed the course of humankind.

4. As you move into the time/space dimension of the Incarnation, ask for the grace of the week: an intimate knowledge of our Lord, who has just become a man for you, that you may love him more deeply and follow him more closely.

5. As you are contemplating the movement from eternity to time, a sort of triptych develops in your imagination, a picture in three parts: the Trinity—three divine persons [106]; the world—all the people on the earth [107]; Nazareth—Mary and the angel [108]. Try to see all of these persons, to hear what they are saying, and to observe what they are doing. As you reflect on this, draw profit from it.

6. When in your prayer God becomes incarnate, speak to him and to our lady, his mother, begging the grace to follow and imitate him more closely.

In coming to know Christ more and in growing in intimacy with him, you cannot isolate the Lord from his social environment. Thus, too, as you reflect upon yourself to draw fruit from the contemplations, your own social milieu in its broad perspective as well as in its particular way of touching you should provide the setting.

7. When your conversation is drawing to a close, finish with an Our Father.

8. Do the reflection, jotting it down.

Second Exercise. Ignatius suggests going to the Nativity for the second exercise, but he says that other mysteries may be added according to the individual retreatant [162]. If the retreatant is a woman, it is often good to have her contemplate the Visitation; some men profit from this mystery also. If the Visitation is given as the second exercise, the Nativity may become the third exercise. Then the fourth is a repetition of the first three exercises, and the fifth is the application of the senses. Or the Nativity may be used as the first exercise of the second day, preserving on the first day the rhythm Ignatius introduces of only two mysteries, one or two repetitions, and an application of the senses for each day.

The director guides the retreatant as follows:

1. Use the preparatory prayer.

2. Ask for the grace: to know Jesus more intimately, to love him more deeply, and to follow him more closely.

3. Read the Scripture, Luke 1:39-52. With Gabriel having indicated to Mary her cousin's pregnant condition, Mary goes to Elizabeth to help her. Visualize Mary on the way to Ain Karim and the house where Elizabeth lives. Even go with her so that you can understand what these women felt; walk in their sandals for a while. Listen to them, and observe them. Notice the interdependence necessary for the word of the Incarnation to spread. There is selflessness and receptivity, and something "bigger than Nazareth" here. Apply this to our day.

4. Talk with Mary and Elizabeth, with John the Baptist, with Jesus, asking for the grace you desire, even as you are becoming aware of its implications. Close with an Our Father.

5. Jot down reflections.

Third Exercise. Unless held for the second day, the mystery of the Nativity is introduced by the director [110-117].

1. Use the preparatory prayer.

2. Ask for the same grace: to know Jesus more intimately, to love him more deeply, to follow him more closely [113].

3. With a census ordered, Mary and Joseph make the decision to go together from Nazareth to Bethlehem despite the condition of Mary [111]. It is reasonable that they take somebody with them to be of help if the baby is born while they are away from home. Might you be that person?

4. See in your imagination the way to Bethlehem, the place where Christ is born; this is your opportunity to make it the way you really think it could have been. Giving your imagination over to God, let God draw you into the mystery [112]; [114-116].

See what Mary and Joseph are doing: you have gone with them to Bethlehem; now be of assistance to them. Listen to them, and talk with them. Really observe all that is going on, especially the poverty in which Christ is born. Consider what life will have to offer to this newborn Christ—labors, hunger, thirst, heat, cold, insults, outrages, death on a cross. Notice how God identifies with the poor, the transient and the dispossessed by the very circumstances of this birth. Yet God does not turn from the wealthy (the Magi), who would be open to God, even seek God out. There is a real international and cross-cultural dimension to this mystery. Yes, every economic bracket is touched by the birth of Jesus. Has there been a carry-over into our day? Does the fact that God became human for us touch the lived reality of society?

5. God chose to enter into this life for you! Talk with God about all of this [117]. Close the prayer period with an Our Father.

6. Jot down your reflections.

Fourth Exercise. This prayer period is a repetition of the first three exercises.

1. Use the same preparatory prayer.

2. Ask for the grace: to know Jesus more intimately, to love him more deeply, to follow him more closely.

3. Let your imagination carry you from before the Incarnation to the Nativity. Experience the movement from meeting with the Eternal Trinity to Nazareth and then to Bethlehem and the cave where Jesus is born. Turn to those parts of the previous contemplations that gave consolation, and savor them again; to those parts that gave greater spiritual insight, and let that insight deepen; to those parts that gave desolation, and confront the reason for that desolation.

4. Talk with the Trinity or Jesus or Mary and Joseph, as you are led to do. Close with an Our Father.

5. Do the reflection, jotting down as before.

Fifth Exercise. The fifth exercise is an application of the senses, one that should be done with a minimum of reasoning. It should be a simple entering into the mystery being contemplated, with the senses wide open. Imagination can stimulate the senses to act, for example, smelling a flower, feeling cold or pain, and so on. Give your imagination over to God; let it serve you to make you present to the Gospel with very little activity on your part, rather with quiet receptivity. Let your senses draw you into the mystery in a participative way.

1. Use the preparatory prayer.

2. Ask for the same grace as in the other four exercises.

3. Once again recall the time from before the Incarnation to the Nativity, and be with the Eternal Trinity, following the movement through the Incarnation to Bethlehem and the cave where Jesus is born.

4. Interact with the Divine Persons and with the others whom you are contemplating. Close with an Our Father.

5. Note your reflections.

The progression of the five exercises, from presentation of new mysteries to repetitions and finally to the application of the senses, is meant to be a movement into simpler and deeper prayer. Using the senses can be a help in distractions to draw you back to the mystery in any of these prayer periods.

Actually, Ignatius mentions twice [129], [133] that adaptation may be made in favor of four exercises rather than five exercises each day, especially from the second day to the fourth day inclusive. It would seem that extra energy may be needed for the upcoming Meditation on the Two Standards and what follows.

Notes [127-131] are very helpful. Thus, the retreatant is reminded to read "only the mystery that I am immediately to contemplate," and that one's way of spending the day should correspond to the material to be contemplated. For example, the matter of darkening one's room: the retreatant begins to take over his or her own direction, according to the mystery to be contemplated. This last directive, then, becomes a simple exercise of the third paragraph of the First Principle and Foundation [23].

The Second Day [132]

First Exercise. Presentation in the Temple, Luke 2:22-39.
Second Exercise. Flight into Exile in Egypt, Matt. 2:13-18
Third Exercise. Repetition
Fourth Exercise. Application of Senses

or

First Exercise. The Nativity, Luke 2:1-14
Second Exercise. Presentation in the Temple, Luke 2:22-39
Third Exercise. Repetition
Fourth Exercise. Application of Senses

The Third Day and Those That Follow [134]

According to the text of Ignatius, adapt as seems best [162]. In presenting the exercises, the director follows the same manner of presentation as on the first day, but he or she becomes more and more brief. The director must take care not to homilize or to interpret for the directee the Scripture to be contemplated [2]. One must be cautious in the call to the social dimension that the retreatant be left free. It is the prerogative of God to deal directly with the individual and to give the spiritual insights meant specifically for this retreatant. For the director to be verbose only interferes with the action of the Spirit. Thus, it will often be the case that once the retreatant grasps the meaning of contemplation, the director will simply offer the chapter and verses of Scripture to be contemplated, without further elaboration.

The Fourth Day

While continuing to contemplate Christ's life the retreatant begins to get his or her own life in perspective. If this is a retreat of election, it is at this point that the retreatant begins to take a look at the life choices to be discerned. If it is a retreat being made to deepen one's life choice and to move toward living it more fully, the material on Choice of a Way of Life need not be entertained in detail [135], [169-189]. However, it is well to have the retreatant confront his or her life choice so that confirmation, with a fresh and deeper choosing, can be experienced as part of the retreat. If doubts arise in the retreatant regarding vocation, they should not be skirted but should be dealt with in the context of the retreat.

The classic meditations on the Two Standards [136148] and the Three Classes of Persons [149-157] and later on the Three Kinds of Humility [165-168] are to be used whether or not it is a retreat of election.

The Two Standards [136-148]

A kind of Kingdom meditation again, this one places an accent on tactics so as to expose the enemy. The following schema might help the director:

Values of Satan	Self-definition	Values of Christ
Riches: Satan wants self-definition—individual or nation—to rest on manipulation of goods and on manipulation of others to attain goods.	What is possessed defines me or my country: infant stage of human growth.	*Poverty*: freedom from self-definition or national identity in terms of possessions; freedom in union with Christ poor.
Honor: Satan wants self-definition—individual or nation—to rest on the notion of self-validation through depending on the esteem of others.	Approval of others defines me or my country; adolescent stage of human growth.	*Humiliations*: freedom from self-definition in terms of validation by others, freedom in union with Christ insulted.
Pride: Satan wants self-definition—individual or nation—to rest on one's own independence or on national supremacy, even armed supremacy.	Self-sufficiency defines me or my country; adult stage of human growth.	*Humility*: freedom from independence or supremacy as the essence of self-validation, freedom in union with Christ humble, beloved of God.

Keeping this schema in mind can help the director in presenting the meditation on the Two Standards.

The word "standard" can hold two meanings in this text:

1. *Flag of battle*—Ignatius uses military language, indicating a particular army with which one sides; "Christ calls and wants all beneath his standard" [137].

2. *Value system*—Satan presents the value system, or the "standard," of the world: riches—honor—pride. Society reinforces this system. On the other hand, Christ presents his "standard," or value system: poverty—humiliations—humility. Diametrically opposed, society persecutes those who hold his standard.

Although as a meditation the Two Standards is somewhat of a digression from the contemplating that the retreatant has been doing, the prayer period has the same format with which the retreatant has become familiar.

1. Use the same preparatory prayer [46].

2. Enter into the setting. Realize that Christ wants all under his standard, wants us to live in his value system, which leads to freedom and life. On the other hand, Lucifer wants all under his standard, wants us to live in his value system, which leads to bondage and death [137].

   Visualize two battlefields: one is near Jerusalem, the Holy City that symbolizes our salvation; Jesus Christ is Commander-in-Chief. The other is near Babylon, symbol of evil, where Lucifer commands the enemy [138].

3. Ask for the grace: knowledge of the devil's tactics, of the world's value system, and the help to guard myself against them; and also knowledge of the true life exemplified in Christ, and the grace to imitate him [139].

4. The director would do well to read over with the retreatant the text of Ignatius [140-146], contrasting the violent vocabulary used to describe the standard of Satan and the gentle, inviting vocabulary used to describe the standard of Christ,

respecter of our freedom. It can be helpful to elaborate on the last paragraph of number 146, using the schema given above. Bringing all this into our own milieu can occur through some questions such as the following:

How do I experience the value system of the world attracting me, catching me, holding me in its grasp? What characterizes my behavior as I experience this? What about the "collective me"? How do we buy into this value system as a society, a nation; where is it all leading? How does the Lord manage to cut through all this and get to my attention or touch our national conscience? How does he lead me, if I (we) let him, into his value system? What will happen if I really let his value system get inside of me and direct all my behavior? Sometimes I must beg for the grace to even *want* to imitate him this closely.

5. A triple colloquy is suggested because the matter is difficult and challenging [147].

6. The usual reflection period follows [77].

This exercise is to be prayed twice. It is followed by one or two repetitions and then the meditation on the Three Classes of Persons—a seemingly simple meditation which offers a real challenge to the directee, including its note at the end.

Three Classes of Persons [149-157]

1. Use the preparatory prayer.

2. Enter into the setting. Visualize the communion of saints gathered before our Lord. Take your place among them and listen to Christ telling a story; let him look deeply into your eyes, into your soul, as he tells it [151]. He describes three types of persons, comparable to three groups with special interests, even three nations. Having acquired a great sum of money, each of them has become attached to it, and they now desire to get rid of the attachment they feel for the

money [150]. Although money is the object of attachment in the story, it could be anything; Ignatius simply starts where evil gets in first, namely possessions.

3. Ask for the grace: "to choose what is more for the glory of His Divine Majesty and the salvation of my soul" [152]. Note the presence once again of the First Principle and Foundation [23].

4. The director may tell the story briefly: [153] *The First Person* wants to get rid of the attachment, and says to self, "One day I must do something about this." But this person never gets around to it and, therefore, dies with the attachment. I sometimes find myself like this, don't I? [154] *The Second Person* wants to get rid of the attachment and sets out to do it. But the very attachment is blinding, and this person begins to figure out how the money can be used for good things: perhaps it can be invested and the interest used for the poor. This person exemplifies "having our cake and eating it too," by sort of baptizing the attachment; thus the person does not rid self of the attachment. I sometimes find myself like this person too. [155] *The Third Person* wants to get rid of the attachment, seeking the Lord's will in regard to keeping the money or not. This person does not act precipitously. Neither getting rid of the money immediately nor using it for an investment, this one acts as though not possessing it at all, while discerning the will of God in this matter.

5. A threefold colloquy is again prescribed [156]. In fact, Ignatius sends the retreatant back to the colloquies of the Two Standards [147]. He has purpose in this, wanting to tie together one's desire with the effort needed to bring that desire to reality. Ignatius provides a special direction for praying the colloquies in the Note [157]. Sometimes a retreatant finds such repugnance to that Note that there is even a block to understanding it. He or she might feel that to beg

our Lord for the opposite of an attachment is speaking untruthfully, since we can only be attached to what we consider to be good for us. The director can encourage the retreatant by pointing out that in praying in this way we admit to ourselves and to God that our whole nature rebels against asking to be separated from the object of our attachment. But actually we are trying to give in to our deeper desire, a much more graced desire, to choose whatever is more for God's honor and glory and for one's greater life in God.

6. Do the reflection and jotting.

The Fifth and Following Days

With the fifth day the retreatant resumes contemplations on the life of Jesus. The meditations of the preceding days often prove to deepen one's response to the Lord in these subsequent contemplations.

Ignatius prescribes that a mystery be contemplated twice, followed by two repetitions, and finally the application of the senses [159]. He also says that the retreatant, "according to his progress, may lengthen or shorten this Week" [162]. The fifth day exemplifies the format:

> *First Exercise.* Baptism of Jesus
> *Second Exercise.* Baptism of Jesus
> *Third Exercise.* Repetition
> *Fourth Exercise.* Repetition
> *Fifth Exercise.* Application of the senses

With each contemplation, the retreatant uses the triple colloquy. For this, Ignatius sends one back to the Three Classes of Persons [156], which in turn sends one back to the Two Standards [147]. Or the retreatant may be praying "*Agere Contra,*" according to Note [157]. Cf. [16].

During the fifth day and those that follow, the Three Kinds of Humility should be thought over from time to time. If one desires to attain the third kind of humility, then he or she continues to use the triple colloquy.

Three Kinds of Humility [165-168]

This consideration is a movement from basic union with Christ to intimacy with him and then to identification with him, even in externals. Note [168] indicates that we can only desire the third kind of humility. We cannot attain it on our own; it must be granted to us by God, who likewise gives us the desire.

For this reason, many directors are low-key when presenting this exercise. It is sufficient for the retreatant to be introduced to the matter and to ponder it as it recurs to the mind off and on during the day. There may well be a growing desire, initiated by the Lord, to conform one's life more and more to the Christ being contemplated in a particular mystery during four or five prayer periods each day.

What this means concretely for a particular retreatant becomes clearer as the retreat progresses, If the retreatant has consistently been moved by the Lord to dwell on his or her social reality, the implications for the different degrees of humility can become very clear and even frightening. The director must not be manipulative but may suggest that the retreatant pray for courage and the grace to be as close as possible to the Lord at all times. Director and retreatant should continue to note the word "equally" in the second and third kinds of humility [166] [167].

Moving Toward the Election

If the retreatant has a copy of the *Spiritual Exercises*, it can be a help in this Second Week to have one retrace his or her steps so far in the Exercises by reading in a continuous manner certain key passages: [21] Purpose of the Spiritual Exercises; [23] First Principle and Foundation; [53] Colloquy after meditation on sin: "What has been my lived response to Christ?"; [95] Kingdom of Christ; [97] Third point of Kingdom: interior kingdom; [98] "Eternal Lord of all things . . ."; [146] Standard of Christ; [147] Triple Colloquy; [155] Third Class of Persons—choosing the "more"; [157] Note on Third Class; [167] Third Kind of Humility; [169] Introduction to Making a Choice of a Way of Life: its last paragraph; [189] Reformation of One's Way of Living in his or her State of Life.

Aids to the Right Order of One's Life

In order to assist a person to come to the election, that to which the Lord is calling now as an effectual way to direct one's life more surely to him, the following four questions might be presented for consideration in between prayer periods. These questions are best given with the contemplation on the Call of the Apostles, suggested for the seventh day.

1. Why am I in my specific mode of life at this time, that is, religious, clerical, married, single lay life?

2. What does this mean for me in its greatest depth?

3. What are the obstacles within me to a full living out of this call?

4. What concrete measures do I find the Lord calling me to in order to overcome these obstacles?

There should be a basic theme running through a person's retreat that begins to take shape at about this time, a recurring conviction that offers the power to regulate, to order one's life. The director will encourage the retreatant to specify this conviction in the simplest way possible, assisting him or her in this during the next few days until the retreatant is satisfied that the election arrived at is truly that to which the Lord is calling at this time.

Retreat of Election

If one truly is Making a Choice of a Way of Life, the director should be exceptionally familiar with numbers 167-188. The salient points from this material are quite clear. The retreatant must strive to make his or her choice simple, based on the end for which each of us has been created. The person must choose the means to this end, avoiding the temptation to turn this around because of inordinate attachment. One's first aim should be to seek to respond to God and then to discover the best way as an individual to do this. The retreatant is not even considering here the choice between good and evil. One is concerned with making a graced choice among matters that are either indifferent or good in themselves.

There are three times when a choice may be made:

1. When it is obvious the way God is leading.

2. When it is not immediately obvious, but the retreatant does experience movements of consolation and desolation when considering the various choices. The director is extremely important at this point to assist the retreatant in the testing of the movements.

3. When the retreatant is so tranquil that he or she experiences no movements at all when considering the various choices. At this time, thinking as well as praying is essential. Begging for the constant grace to become and remain indifferent, the retreatant asks for clarity about what would be for God's greater honor and glory. Then he or she begins to weigh the matter with care and fidelity, listing the advantages and the disadvantages for each alternative. The choice is made of that alternative which has the weightier reasons for it. The retreatant presents this choice to God for confirmation by God's giving peace regarding it.

If the retreatant needs added help in making a choice proceeding from the love of God, he or she may reflect upon any of three questions:

1. If I were directing somebody else, what would I advise that person?

2. If I were on my death bed, which choice would I wish I had made?

3. If I were standing before the Lord in judgment, which choice would I wish I had made?

Then the retreatant makes the choice and offers it to God for confirmation.

Sixth Day Onward

From the sixth day until the end of the Second Week [161], mysteries in the public life of Our Lord are suggested by Ignatius, one to be contemplated each day. As the director grows in knowledge of the retreatant, he or she makes the decision about which of these mysteries to present or which mysteries are better substituted for this retreatant [162].

There is a logical progression to those in [161] leading from the call to follow Christ [275] through the demands of this venture [278], to the risks involved [280], and finally to the results, as one contemplates the events leading up to the Passion [285], [287]. The final days of the Second Week, as a movement toward the contemplation of Christ's Passion in the Third Week, should include such things as the Raising of Lazarus, the Anointing at Bethany, and Palm Sunday. As the retreatant is drawn deeply into each of these contemplations, the director notices a growing readiness, even the desire, to contemplate Christ in his Passion. The retreatant is now ready to move into the Third Week.

Chapter 6

The Third Week

Dynamics of the Third Week [190-209]

Within the dynamic of the *Spiritual Exercises,* the goal of the Third Week is to confirm the election of the retreatant through the grace of deepened passionate personal love of and compassion for the suffering Jesus, so that I desire to go all the way to Calvary with him in laboring to bring the Kingdom to be. The *id quod volo,* or grace to be prayed for, is intense compassion (compati: "to suffer with"), as detailed in the third prelude of the second and following exercises: "sorrow with Christ in sorrow, anguish with Christ in anguish, tears and deep grief because of the great affliction Christ endures for me" [203]. I pray for a profoundly felt interior participation in the sufferings of Jesus. In the continuing dynamic of the meditations on the Kingdom of Christ [91-99] and on the Two Standards [136-149], one is praying to be transformed into an active participant in Christ's saving of humanity continuing today in the Church, according to one's own specific Christian vocation and retreat election.

It is striking that in the *Autobiographical Directory,* Ignatius says that if a person already has a Christian vocation, the director might propose that one make the election on the following: (1) when the divine service is equal and there will be no guilt or harm to the neighbor, to desire injuries and humiliations and to be held in contempt totally with Christ, in order to wear his livery, imitating him in this part of his Cross; or (2) to be disposed to suffer patiently for the love of Christ whatever similar thing comes into one's life.[1]

The compassion prayed for is that coming from passionate personal love of the suffering Jesus. It is *not* comprehension, which is so far beyond us.

Father Laplace suggests a helpful image: it is like the feeling of a child watching its parents cry. The child does not understand the world of sorrow of adults, but he or she does take their hands. Feeling the hand of their child in theirs consoles the suffering parents. This is probably what compassion with Jesus suffering means for us. Remaining near this suffering will break something in our hearts, as happens in a child initiated into suffering. He or she can never see the world in the same way again.

Experience has shown that the exercises of the Third Week sometimes bring the grace, if not yet given, of the desire for the Third Kind of Humility [167-168]. Progression toward this depth of personal love of Jesus might be described as: *commitment* to Christ (First Week); growing into *intimacy* with Christ (Second Week); which leads one to desire *identification* with Christ in His suffering (Third Week).

The First Contemplation [190-199]

The entry way into the Passion is the Eucharist. The third prelude [193] recalls the *id quod volo* of the first exercise of the First Week [48]. However, the focus now is on Jesus—the depth of his love shown in taking on the weight of my sins. Thus, the grade of sorrow and shame prayed for now is not, as it was in the First Week, for what my sins *are,* but for what my sins caused Jesus to suffer.

---

1. *Directoria Exercitiorum Spiritualium, 1540-1599* (Rome: Historical Institute of the Society of Jesus, 1955), #23, 0. 78.

The six points of Ignatian contemplation of the Third Week [194-197], and the successive repetitions and application of the senses [204], are intended to lead the retreatant into a slow rhythm of looking *long* and allowing the mystery to penetrate one's heart.

The fifth point is designed to bring the realization that the suffering of Jesus "for my sins" is by his own free act of expressing in his body the love of God for us. This does not *happen* to him; he freely wills it as a priestly act. A helpful analogy for the divinity "hiding itself" as stated in this point— namely, that it is not felt—is the experience one has of not actually feeling grace during desolation, although only the reality of grace makes it possible to live and act in such dryness of faith. Jesus suffered in the kind of agony of felt absence and darkness that we experience [196].

The sixth point recalls the colloquy of the first exercise of the First Week [53]; but "what I ought to do for Christ" has become focused through the prayer of the Kingdom of Christ [91-99], of the Two Standards [136-148], of the Third Kind of Humility [167], and of my election into the mission to which I am sent in the Church, thus, now to labor and suffer with Jesus to bring the Kingdom to be [197].

The closing colloquy again focuses the movements and insights experienced during the entire prayer period, and the retreatant may well feel moved to a Triple Colloquy [199] or perhaps to the use of the *agere contra* [157]; cf. [16].

The change in the Additional Directions once more is meant to arrange the environment as a help to one's being open to the grace being sought [206]. The sixth Additional Direction brings forward the whole dynamic of contemplating the human life of Jesus initiated by the third point of the contemplation of the Nativity, "born in extreme poverty, and after many labors . . . insults and outrages, he might die on the cross, and all this for me" [116].

Rules With Regard to Eating [210-217]

At the end of the exercises of the Third Week, Ignatius proposes Rules with Regard to Eating. These Rules are really a concrete application of the practical principle of the First Principle and Foundation, the ordering of one's actions in daily life to God [23]. He states their purpose as "to secure for the future due order in the use of food." The placement of these rules at the end of the Third Week seems aimed toward enabling the exercitant in the light of his or her own election to order life to God, recognizing that such ordering often will require denial of disorderly appetites. The contemplation of Jesus in the mysteries of his passion will have provided powerful motivation to the person to practice the necessary self-denial.

These Rules, then, are really a model for ordering all the details of one's life to God. Ignatius probably focused on eating as the model because during his time gluttony was very common. This example is relevant today, too, when there is a great deal of overeating and of alcoholic abuse in many of the cultures where the Exercises are made. The director should point out, according to the needs of each retreatant, how the principles given in these Rules can be effective means to help one to order such things as use of time, of recreation, of television, of reading, and so on, always to God.

By using the staple food of his time and place, namely, bread, Ignatius points out how that is not so likely to excite inordinate appetite [210]; if he had lived in Asia, the staple would have been rice—and so today, that of each culture must be given similar application. However, the normal drink at meals was wine; so, he points out the need "to consider carefully what would be helpful and therefore to be permitted; and what would be harmful, and to be avoided" [211]. This is a concrete application of the principle in the First Principle and Foundation for the use of all creatures: "Hence, one is to make use of them in as far as they help one in the attainment of the end, and one must rid self of them in as far as they prove a hindrance" [23].

More delicate foods—in Spanish, *manjares,* which means delicacies—can more easily lead one to eat excessively, and so not to be ordered to the praise and reverence and service of God. Thus, common sense will aid a person to order appetite through retrenchment [212]. Through deliberate retrenchment, an individual may experience consolations that will enable one quickly to discern ordered uses of these things.[2] At the least, by experience one will learn what is ordered use, "the mean one should observe" [213].

Ongoing growth in the attitudes of Jesus through continual contemplation of him will gradually enable a person to have a pervasive consciousness of ordering all to God, which will overcome any disordered tendency to self-gratification [214-215]. Thus, one will remain on guard against strong disordered desires and will possess the self-control required [216]. Finally, Ignatius encourages the person to take practical measures to grow in wisdom in ordering his or her life through reflection on experience and planning for the future. Here, a great help can be the daily use of the particular examination of conscience [24-31], as well as using the *agere contra* technique [12], [16], [157], [350].

Using the principles of the Rules with Regard to Eating, the director can help the exercitant to prepare for living out in the future in daily life the behavioral consequences of commitment to order everything in one's life to the praise and reverence and service of God.

The Prayer of the Third Week

Ignatius seems to take it for granted, because of the dynamic of gradual simplification of prayer during the Second Week, that the retreatant will enter the Third Week ready for the prayer of simple presence appropriate for the Passion. A simple image draws the mind and the heart. Thus, he shows great flexi-

---

2. Cf. "Rules for Discernment of Spirits II," in Part IV.

bility as he offers the suggestion of contemplating the mysteries in succession, without repetitions and the application of the senses [209].

During the Third Week the function of the Additional Observations for establishing the proper environment—bodily and psychological conditions for prayer—is more important than ever [206], since this prayer requires deep recollection and a profound unity of atmosphere.

Father Laplace reflects that one's prayer should now become more passive, more a *resting* in the feelings called forth by the scenes, such as compassion, wonder, sorrow, love. A person is placed before a great mystery and senses that through it, if we come to realize it, one will reach the very core of prayer. However, often precisely at this moment, the retreatant experiences great difficulty in praying: distractions, dryness, and the impossibility of fixing attention. Nevertheless, now less than ever does one want to abandon prayer, having some glimpse of its hidden riches. But one feels like a person witnessing a horrible drama with indifference. Desiring to be profoundly moved, he or she, in fact, feels truly ill at ease. Confronting these scenes that should be true sources of light, all one feels is lack of understanding and difficulties of spirit. In the very effort to pray, the individual feels empty and tense. If one feels something like this when contemplating the Passion, one, as a matter of fact, is achieving its fruit.

I must continue to pray and to experience desolation. The present feeling is neither that of tender and falsifying emotion nor of discouragement. I know by faith that I am the recipient of a personal infinite love. What I am suffering is the awareness of loving so little this Jesus, who is deserving of absolute love. I desire a change of heart, a growth in love. Consequently, this is a good suffering. It situates me in truth before Jesus. It is an appeal to the Holy Spirit, so that some day when God wills it, my feelings truly will be reached by the Passion. One moment of such true consolation will make up for all the years of power-less waiting for the Lord.

The difficulty of praying the Passion is twofold. First of all, its object makes it difficult. It is Jesus suffering his Passion who occupies our entire consciousness. This is the most selfless prayer. However, a prayer that no longer refers to ourselves is necessarily more austere. Even though we shall, at times, have insights concerning our own lives and actions [197], this prayer essentially is simply contemplating Jesus suffering for love of us—looking *long* at him in his Passion. This prayer is rich in results for us personally and for our apostolate, because it unites us with Jesus selflessly in love. Secondly, this prayer is difficult because of the unity of atmosphere that it requires. Throughout the entire day, it is an exercise of the presence of God and an effort not to have any other thought than that of the Passion of Jesus. But the more delicate the prayer, the more distractions tend to flock in. We must simply let these fall peacefully and then return to the contemplation of Jesus suffering: "I JUST WANT TO BE WITH YOU."

Moving Into the Third Week [190-209]

Approaches to the Third Week

The Third Week of the Spiritual Exercises presents its own kind of challenge. The retreatant has undoubtedly given prayer-ful attention to the Passion many times in his or her life. But this time it will be different. The growing intimacy in knowl-edge, love, and service of Jesus that has been the grace of the Second Week brings one face-to-face with the consequences of living out such a reality in a world that is not oriented toward Christ. The most usual mind-set in the retreatant approaching this week is the sincere desire to suffer *with* Jesus as he goes through his Passion and death, to be compassionate with him during these most difficult moments he endures.

The grace of the week as expressed in the *Exercises* is nuanced somewhat differently, however. It is to ask for sorrow, compassion, and shame because the Lord is going to his suffering *"for my sins"* [193]. This grace will be given as the individual retreatant will profit most from it; thus the expectation with which one enters the week is often met in quite a different manner than anticipated.

It is not unusual for this week to be extremely dry in prayer. Thus, Ignatius urges the retreatant "with great effort to strive . . . to labor through all the points" [195]. It does not come easy, and there may be various reasons for this. One could be that the retreatant has come through some very exacting and psychologically draining days just prior to this. Another is that the retreatant is asking to feel with Christ what he experienced, and it could well be that the prayer of Christ himself was extremely dry at this time: "My God, my God, why have you forsaken me?" It seems unimaginable that Jesus was drawn by much consolation through his Passion. Still another cause of the dryness in prayer might be connected with the nuance mentioned above, "for my sins." It is much more difficult to be with someone in true compassion when we are aware of being the cause of the suffering.

There are two indications that a person is ready for the Third Week:

1. The election: In the classic retreat of election [169188], the person has arrived at a point of decision, which will be confirmed during the contemplation of the Passion. In a retreat of reformation of life [189], the retreatant has come to an understanding of what the Lord is asking and is responding with an open-ended "yes." It must be noted, however, that clarity regarding the election/reformation of life does not always come with the Third Week.

2. The retreatant manifests a deepening desire for union with Christ, no matter what, and usually experiences a desire, al-

though sometimes accompanied by hesitation and even fear, to move with Christ into a contemplation of his Passion, and to glimpse what this will mean concretely after the retreat. There is evidence of some movement toward the Third Degree of Humility, at least the person wants to desire this grace. When expressing the desire to suffer with Christ, not just in prayer time but in the experience of everyday life, the retreatant may say, "I simply can't desire suffering, even to be like Jesus." Here the director must explain that one does not, of course, ask for suffering or desire suffering for its own sake. One's desire, one's whole thrust is to become so identified with Christ that the suffering is inevitable. The concentration is on the person of *more* Jesus, not on the consequences, although in embracing union with Jesus, one is also embracing the consequences. These consequences will be experienced in the lived reality of every day, not only in imagination or prayer where one is safely away from misunderstanding or rejection or imprisonment or death.

The Third Week is an experience that will test the authenticity of these desires. In the Colloquies of this week, one actually brings the fruit of the Second Week to the Lord, praying for the grace to be able to carry it out. Thus, the fruit of the Second Week can be confirmed through one's praying these colloquies.

Because Ignatius himself suggests a variety of ways of going about the Third Week [209], directors differ in their approaches to these days, even a single director varying the approach with different directees, more so than with any week other than the First. I wish now to offer some ways of presenting the Third Week to the retreatants, based both on varying numbers of days and on differing approaches.

1. *One Director might Proceed according to the text, using seven days.*

By following numbers 190-208 in the *Spiritual Exercises,* the retreatant moves consecutively and chronologically through the Passion during six days, with a seventh to contemplate the entire Passion. Although Ignatius proposes the repetitions and the application of senses on most of these days, it is notable that on this final day he drops them in favor of one's considering "as frequently as possible through this whole day" [208. Seventh Day] Christ's burial and the weariness of Mary and the disciples.

2. *Another, beginning with the Last Supper, may plan on five days.*

> FIRST DAY: *Last Supper.* With so much to be contemplated, this material can easily provide four or five prayer periods [205]. One can spend time, for example, on (1) the preparation in secret of the upper room, (2) the washing of the feet, (3) the last discourse of Jesus, (4) the institution of the Eucharist, (5) the dialogues with Judas, Peter, and John. Or, the retreatant might simply move through the contemplation over the entire day, stopping wherever he or she seems to be held in prayer but without definite periods of any specific length of time.

> SECOND DAY: *Agony in Garden.* Referring the retreatant to the Note after the meditation on the Three Classes of Persons [157], the director might suggest that he or she use a single account from each one of the synoptic Gospels for the first three prayer periods, and then make one or two repetitions or the application of senses.

> THIRD DAY: Entire Passion. The entire Passion is contemplated using five prayer periods. If

the director gives to the retreatant the Scripture references already written down, the flow of the contemplation can be facilitated.

Thus, the five contemplations proceed as follows:

- Arrest of Jesus/Jesus before the Sanhedrin
    Matt. 26:47-68
    Mark 14:43-65
    Luke 22:47-53, 63-71
    John 18:1-16, 19-24

- Peter's denial/Judas
    Matt. 26:69-27:10
    Mark 14:66-72
    Luke 22:54-62
    John 18:15-18, 25-27

- Jesus before Pilate
    Matt. 27:11-26
    Mark 15:1-15
    Luke 23:1-25
    John 18:28-19:16

- Crowning with Thorns/Way of the cross
    Matt. 27:27-34
    Mark 15;16-23
    Luke 23:26-31
    John 19:16-17

- Crucifixion and death of Jesus
    Matt. 27:35-66
    Mark 15:24-47
    Luke 23:32-56
    John 19:18-42

FOURTH DAY: *Entire Passion*, contemplated in an unstructured way.

FIFTH DAY: *At the Tomb* [208. Seventh Day].

This day at the tomb is very salutary and can be spent as the apostles might have spent it, with Mary and one another recalling the events of the time they had shared in the life of Jesus. Therefore, some directors suggest to a given retreatant that he or she might wish to take a quiet walk with another retreatant in this manner, if it seems that the person needs some sort of break at this point.

3. *Also comprising five days is another approach:*

FIRST DAY: *Last Supper*
- The Meal and the betrayer
    Matt. 26:17-25
    Mark 14:12-21, 27-31
    Luke 27:7-13, 21-38
    John 13:18-38

- Washing of the feet
    John 13:1-7

- Institution of the Eucharist
    Matt. 26;26-30
    Mark 14:22-26
    Luke 22:14-20

- The Last Discourse
    John 14-17

- A repetition of the entire supper

SECOND DAY: *Farther into the Passion*
- Agony in Garden
- Arrest of Jesus/Jesus before the Sanhedrin
- Peter's denial/ Judas

- Repetition
- The application of senses

THIRD DAY: *Complete the Passion*
- Jesus before Pilate
- Crowning with thorns/Way of the cross
- Crucifixion and death of Jesus
- A repetition
- The application of senses

FOURTH DAY: *Immersed in the Passion,*
In an unstructured way, it might be well to suggest that the retreatant make the way of the Cross this day.

FIFTH DAY: *At the Tomb.*

4. *A director can draw on the different Gospels using four to six days.*

FIRST DAY: *Last Supper and Agony in the Garden*
SECOND DAY: *Entire Passion,* using one Gospel
THIRD DAY: *Same,* using a different Gospel
Possible FOURTH DAY and FIFTH DAY:
Same, using a different Gospel
SIXTH DAY: *At the Tomb*
The director instructs the retreatant to stop wherever God seems to want to spend time with him or her, for as long as God keeps one there. In any case, what seems to be important, rather than covering the Passion in a set number of days, is to be *with* Christ in his Passion as deeply as he draws one into it.

5. *Another can extend the Second Week to eleven days as a fuller preparation for moving toward the Passion* (cf. Second Week).

Thus, the Second Week follows the pattern outlined by Ignatius from the First day through the Seventh Day [101-161]. The Eighth Day is a contemplation of Jesus and Peter "on the waves of the sea" [280]. With the Ninth Day, the director begins to prepare the retreatant for the Passion and the Third Week with the contemplation of the Raising of Lazarus, since it was at this miracle that the Jews became determined to put Jesus to death; used as spiritual reading is Matt. 16:13-17:8. The Tenth Day is a contemplation of the Anointing at Bethany, while The Eleventh Day is a contemplation of Palm Sunday. After a repose day, the director guides the retreatant into the prayer of the Third Week, contemplating the Passion.

I would like to mention a couple of practices regarding the structuring of days that I have discovered assist the retreatant's prayer. When a person has entered deeply into being with Jesus' suffering, it is valuable for the director at a conference to give directions all at once for a couple of days. This both avoids interrupting the flow of the retreatant's prayer and begins to wean him or her away from any dependence on the director. Another suggestion treats that day designated for contemplating "that the most Sacred Body of Christ our Lord remained separated from the soul . . . and the desolation of our Lady . . . and that of the disciples" [208. Seventh Day]. I ask that this day At the Tomb extend from after breakfast until 5:00 pm. If some person needs relief from the retreat, some portion of the day can be spent in taking a walk away from the retreat house with another retreatant, or in some similar activity. Then in the evening I see each retreatant for about fifteen minutes to prepare him or her for the first resurrection mystery, which is to be done at dawn.

Rules With Regard to Eating [210-217]

It seems strange, at first encounter, to find these rules placed within the Third Week. Some persons feel that they were placed here by mistake at some point after Ignatius' own time. Others believe that they belong in the Third Week. As such they call the retreatant to order his or her *whole* life, especially appetites, to the Lord (1 Cor. 10:31). They are geared to union with

Christ in things as common and everyday as eating and drinking. They seem to say: "Keep your mind always on him. Always begin with him. Remain conscious of his presence. Do everything the way you think he would do it."

Some retreatants have found these rules, presented in the Third Week, to be one of the most significant parts of the retreat. The implications for society, affluent or otherwise, can be very rich. Such meaning, not to be rendered explicit by the director, should be allowed to surface as the grace of the Spirit moves the retreatant.

Chapter 7

The Fourth Week

Dynamics of the Fourth Week [218-229] and of the Contemplation to Attain Love of God [230-237]

The goal is through contemplation of the Risen Jesus to be able always to see his victory *in* the cross and, thus, to confirm the commitment to live out one's election, no matter what the cost. Here, we enter into the Paschal Good News, an enormous contrast to, yet in continuity with, the Passion. We see that we enter into the death of Jesus in order to enter into His Resurrection, and this enables us to see his victory in our own experiences of being crucified.

The grace or *id quod volo* asked during this Fourth Week is the grace of an utterly selfless love: "to be glad and rejoice intensely because of the great joy and the glory of Christ our Lord" [221]. It would be normal to feel some pity for any person in great suffering; but to rejoice simply because another has joy, even when I have no other joy than this, can happen only when I deeply love that person. The proper effect of the Fourth Week is consolation, to be what St. Augustine said a Christian should always be: "Alleluia from head to foot."

The true effect of the Resurrection consists above all in the *knowledge of God*: in the Scripture, in the effects of his action on us, and in the Church. This can be considered as a week of formation of the apostle—forming in us the qualities of the

Risen Jesus. The contemplations of the Fourth Week open us to the Holy Spirit forming an apostolic spirit within us: courage, hope, love of the Church, simplicity, humanity, love, and finding God in all things.

For the prayer of the Fourth Week, a very delicate and peaceful silence is required, so that the joy of Jesus can invade us, if God so wills. In a sense, this is an even more self-emptied prayer than is contemplation of the Passion. The considering of the divinity manifesting itself "in the most holy Resurrection and in its true and most sacred effects" focuses the contemplations on the spiritual power of the presence of the Risen Christ: effects in the human spirit, building up the community of the Church, and achieving the Kingdom [223].

The arrangement of the prayer periods follows that of the Third Week [226], [209]. Ignatius says that it is "more in keeping with this Week" to have four exercises a day, rather than five [227]. The stress in the application of the senses is on consolation: "attention and more time is to be given to the more important parts and to points where the soul was more deeply moved and spiritual relish was greater" [227]. The number of points to be considered is left to the retreatant, whom Ignatius expects to be experienced in prayer by now [228]. The Additional Directions are changed to provide environmental support for praying for the *id quod volo* [229].

During the Fourth Week, the director should help the retreatant to pray for a realistic faith in and love of the Church, the community of the faithful whose communion is the Spirit of the Risen Jesus and who incarnationally continue his mission until he comes again.

Father Laplace points out that many of the mysteries given by Ignatius for the Fourth Week stress Christ's forming of his Church: [302] strengthening Peter to be the Rock; [303] from personal presence to communion in his presence; [304] community experience of the Risen Lord; [305] the living tradition of the experience of the Risen Jesus in the faith community; [306]

the primacy of Peter; [307] the universal mission of the Church to proclaim the Good News; [312] forming the Church: disciples sent in the power of the Resurrection; apostolic urgency: filling up Christ until he comes again.

The Contemplation to Attain Love of God [230-237]

The goal of this contemplation is to plunge us into the reality that is love and to learn in the concrete here and now of our lives how to serve and love God in all things. We do not seize this love nor arouse it in ourselves. We pray to receive it, this love that "must descend from above" [184] and which penetrates our hearts. We pray to recognize it in the circumstances of our daily lives.

God can give this grace *on one condition*: that one's heart is truly open and free through the liberation of the Two Standards [136-148], and through commitment to election—that particular form of poverty and of self-giving discovered to be one's own call from the Lord.

This Contemplation is the heart of apostolic spirituality: to be contemplative in action, finding God in all things: to be able always to recognize the Love that surrounds us, the Love in which we are immersed, the Love from which everything comes and to which everything goes.

Ignatius says nothing about the place of this Contemplation within the dynamic movement of the Spiritual Exercises, other than by putting it at the end of the book together with the Three Methods of Prayer [238-260]. For this reason, directors are divided as to whether Ignatius intended the Contemplation to be the climax of the entire movement of the Exercises or simply an important way of praying, to be taught to persons as are the Three Methods of Prayer, not necessarily as part of the retreat. For this reason, too, some directors feel free to introduce the Contemplation at an earlier moment in the movement of the retreat. Whatever the truth may be, there is no doubt that the Contemplation can provide a marvelous final moment to the dynamic of the entire Spiritual Exercises, as well as a powerful way to send the retreatant out to live his or her graces in daily life—finding God in all things, *living* discernment.

The grace sought, or *id quod volo*, is a deep, interior knowledge of God's wonderful works of love ("*mirabilia Dei*"), that can only result in a tremendous surge of love in return [233]. This is perhaps best expressed in the French word for gratitude: *reconnaissance*—"knowing again." From this love will come a life of serving God in all things. One's whole life will be Eucharist—thankful self-giving in return to God, thanksliving.

The first point [234] moves from remembering the gifts of God to all human persons into personal *memory* of God's favors to me, an extended *Magnificat* that leads to the *Suscipe*. The only possible response is love in return, always and in everything: "Take and receive." For this to be, I pray for the one thing necessary—God's love and grace.

The second point [235], through reflection upon the gifts of God, leads to a deeper *understanding* of God's love, and so to an even deeper *Suscipe*.

The third point [236] moves one to a heartfelt *awe* before the wonderful works of God—the Spirit of God working in the universe that groans until God is all in all (Rom. 8:21-22). One's *Suscipe* becomes more intensely felt.

In the fourth point [237], the human *spirit* enters into the life of the Trinity: "all blessings and gifts . . . descending from above." This leads toward an awareness at all times of the presence of the Spirit of God in everything and within me. This is the completion of the ongoing movement of the Spiritual Exercises: all things and myself filled with the presence of the Holy Spirit. The *Suscipe* is all embracing.

Father Laplace has pointed out that we can come to this awareness of the universal presence of the Spirit of God, because:

1. *The Holy Spirit is the interiority of God.* "For the spirit explores everything, even the depths of God's own nature. Among human persons, who knows what a person is but the person's own spirit within one? In the same way, only the spirit of God knows what God is. This is the spirit that we have received from God." (1 Cor. 2:10-11)

2. The Holy Spirit is the interiority of our *spiritual consciousness.* "In the same way, the spirit comes to the aid of our weakness. We do not even know how we ought to pray, but through our inarticulate groans, the spirit is pleading for us, and God who searches our inmost being knows what the spirit means" (Rom. 8:26-27). "Abba, Father! In that cry the spirit of God joins with our spirit in testifying that we are God's children, and, if children, then heirs" (Rom. 8:16). "Surely you know that you are God's temple, where the spirit of God dwells" (1 Cor. 3:16).

3. The *Holy Spirit is the* interiority of all *things.* "The Spirit of the Lord fills the world" (Pentecost Antiphon)

   BLESSED BE THE NAME OF GOD FOREVER FOR ALL THAT GOD HAS WORKED IN US THROUGH JESUS CHRIST IN THE HOLY SPIRIT!

Moving Into the Fourth Week and Concluding the Retreat [218-237]

In presenting this week, a director might prefer to see the retreatants in the afternoon of the day spent "At the Tomb." Besides allowing each one to experience the full effect of the Third Week without anticipating the Fourth Week, it prepares each to begin the Fourth Week at dawn, using nature to assist toward joy with Christ in joy.

The grace to be asked for is joy with Christ in joy. It is not an expectation on the part of Christ that a retreatant must fulfill. Sometimes a retreatant does not feel joy at this time, and then experiences guilt because of a lack of joy; the director should then point out that the retreatant is getting caught in the attitude that he or she makes the joy happen instead of realizing that it is a grace desired. If the retreatant does not receive this grace, it will be helpful to see if he or she is putting obstacles in the way of the grace. Such can be extremely subtle in the retreatant.

If the Lord has drawn the retreatant along the way of the social dimension, that dimension will surely surface again during the Fourth Week and be reinforced.

Should there be only one prayer period before breakfast, it will be on the Apparition of Christ to his Mother [218-225]. Although this is not mentioned in Scripture, it seems unthinkable to Ignatius that Christ would not appear first of all to his mother after rising from the dead [299]. Most retreatants have never considered this before and find it to be a very deep experience.

On each of the next days of the retreat there will be contemplations of two appearances, moving into one repetition and the application of the senses [226-228].

Contemplation to Attain Love of God [230-237]

Ignatius does not make it clear whether this contemplation is a part of the Fourth Week or an addendum to it. Directors treat it in varying ways: some spread it out over the week, using one prayer period each day, either for one point or for the entire *Contemplatio*, as it is sometimes called; others use it in its entirety on the last day only.

The director prepares the retreatant for the prayer in words similar to the following:

1. You will find that the *Contemplatio* summarizes the entire retreat. To open yourself to the fullness of this contemplation, remember that you are involved in an ongoing love relationship with God, both as an individual and as a part of all humankind. Ignatius calls your attention to certain aspects of love in two pre-suppositions, where he stresses: first, there is a natural union of love and action within a person. Love expresses itself in action. And second, that there is a natural union of intercommunion and mutuality between persons who love. Love seeks to share itself with the beloved.[1]

2. The representation of place is familiar to you. As in the Three Classes of Persons [152], you once again "behold self standing in the presence of God our Lord and of the angels and saints." It is yourself and God, surrounded by the whole court of heaven, each one of whom is praying for you [232].

3. Pray for the grace of an intimate knowledge of the many blessings received, during the retreat and otherwise, that gratitude may lead you to love and serve God in all things, with all that this implies. It also refers to a kind of mutuality of love which Ignatius mentioned in the Note above.

4. *The first point recalls the First Week* [234]. It speaks of the blessings of God: creation, redemption, what God has done for you, what God has given you, God's desire to give Godself. Recall the First Week and ponder with great affection all that happened then, including your desire to give yourself to God. Let this desire deepen and express it in the "Take, Lord, and receive." In this prayer, when recognition gives way to love, then love finds expression in concrete surrender.

---

1. For a fuller explanation of this, see Michael J. Buckley, S.J., "The Contemplation to Attain Love," *The Way*, 24 (Spring, 1975), p. 92.

5. The second point recalls the Second Week [235]. God not only gives, but lives within the gift. God does not remain outside of what God has created. Especially reflect on how God dwells in you, giving you the divine presence, the same way as in other creatures, and more. God makes you a temple. In the Second Week you contemplated God's insertion into creation as a human person and the thirty-three years Christ lived among us. You felt Christ's call for you to become intimate with him, to identify with him, until it would be that you live and move and have your being in him. If he gives himself so unreservedly to you, what is your fitting response? "Take, Lord, and receive."

6. The third point recalls the Third Week [236]. Consider how God works and labors for you in all creatures. Not only does God continue to provide for you through them, but God is even mediated to you through them.

> "Earth's crammed with heaven
> And every common bush afire with God
> But only he who sees takes off his shoes
> The rest sit 'round it and pluck blackberries."
> (Elizabeth B. Browning)

Remember Christ's labor of redemption that you contemplated in the Third Week. Remember how you strove to be with him in that labor and the desire to participate in the work of redemption. Let that desire deepen and express itself in "Take, Lord, and receive."

7. The fourth point recalls the Fourth Week [237]. On those days you contemplated Christ the Risen Lord in his role of consoler, promising to fill us with the Spirit [225]. Now you see God as the source, through the Spirit, of all that is within you. Before, you contrasted God's goodness with your meanness [58]. Now you must see that all that is good in you is a participation in God's goodness; your truth is a

participation in God's truth; your justice, in God's justice; your beauty, in God's beauty; and so on. Just as a drop of water is a part of the waterfall, just as a ray of sunlight is a "little bit" of the sun, so your "limited power comes from the supreme and infinite power above" [237]. Since God gives Godself so completely as to draw you to participate in the very being of divinity, let God draw you now to express your desire in "Take, Lord, and receive."

The Last Conference

As a help in moving out of the retreat, a director may want to discuss briefly some of the following things according to the needs of each retreatant: post-retreat shock and noise; loss of supportive structure; frustration and "let down"; movement out of solitude, thus need for solitude; prayer; spiritual direction; particular examen of consciousness; dynamic memory, continuing to recall special graced moments in my life; bringing graces of retreat forward to next retreat; warding off elitism; ecclesial spirituality: read Documents of Vatican II; the social dimensions of peace and justice to which the Church calls.

The conference might close with one or several readings from Scripture as a prayer for the retreatant. Some fitting ones include:

Exod: 33:12-17:	I will go with you from this place.
Jer. 29:11-15:	I know well the plans I have in mind for you.
Acts 20:31-32:	I commend you now to the Lord.
Eph. 3:14-21:	I pray that God will bestow on you

Some retreatants find it difficult to end the retreat, having built a deep relationship with the director. In these cases especially, it is well for the director to mission the retreatant with a blessing.

"Go now, in the name of the Lord."

PART III

Commentaries on Ignatius' Rules

Chapter 8

Rules for Discernment

Rules for Discernment of Spirits I [313-327]

Ignatius presumes that a retreatant will experience movements of consolation and desolation during the Exercises [6-10]. Thus, the director must understand consolation and desolation to be able to help the person discern their origin, so that he or she may integrate these into the movement toward God through the Exercises. For this reason, Ignatius provides two sets of Rules for the Discernment of Spirits, the first appropriate to the First Week [313-327], the second appropriate to the Second Week [328-336]. These rules are both a guide for the director and an instrument for helping the exercitant to grow in the art of spiritual discernment, rules presented by the director when there are signs indicating need for them [8-10]. Because of the importance of these rules in directing the Exercises, it seems necessary within a *Handbook* such as this one to offer somewhat detailed commentaries on them.[1]

Key Element in Spirituality

From the beginning, it is well to recall that spiritual discernment is not a "Jesuit" thing, even though many people have become aware of it through the Spiritual Exercises. Rather, dis-

---

1. Helpful reading matter for the director: Michael J. Buckley, S.J., "Rules for the Discernment of Spirits," *The Way*, Supplement 20 (Autumn, 1973), pp. 19-37. See also my next chapter, "Rules for Discernment of Spirits II."

cernment is the key element in Christian spirituality since its origin; it precisely concerns concrete discovery of the actual word of God in every situation calling one to live love here and now. Spiritual discernment enables a person to see and choose and do the "will of God" at every moment. This is why, beginning with Scripture[2] and going throughout the tradition of Christian spirituality from its earliest expressions, discernment is recognized as the crucial graced act for growth in the life of the Spirit.[3]

In writing his Rules for Discernment of Spirits Ignatius simply entered into that tradition, fifteen hundred years old by then. His own singular contribution to the tradition was to give an excellent practical method for individual discernment in the *Spiritual Exercises* and for communal discernment in the "Deliberation of the First Fathers," through which, in 1539, he and his companions discerned that God called them to found the Society of Jesus.[4]

However, the Rules for Discernment of Spirits in the Spiritual Exercises can be traced through the tradition back to the Sixth Mandatum of the Shepherd of Hermas (c. 140-150 A.D.), and their basic content can be found in the writings of Martin Luther who received the same tradition.[5] The difference between

---

2. For an excellent, documented study of spiritual discernment in Scripture, see Gerard Therrien, C.Ss.R., *Le Discernment dans les ecrits pauliens* (Paris: J. Gabalda, 1973).

3. Cf. "Discernment des esprits," "Discernment of Spirits," trans. Sr. Innocentia Richards, in *Dictionnaire de spiritualite,* (Collegeville, MN: The Liturgical Press, 1970). See also, Fr. Dingjan, O.S.B., *Discretio: les origines patristiques et monastiques de la doctrine sur la prudence chez saint Thomas d'Aquin* (Assen: Van Gorcum and Co., N.V., 1967).

4. For a translation of this Deliberation, see my "Making an Apostolic Community of Love" (St. Louis: Institute of Jesuit Sources, 1970), Appendix I, pp. 187-194. For development of the Ignatian contribution to the tradition of discernment, see my two studies in *Studies in the Spirituality of Jesuits.* "Ignatian Discernment," vol. II, No. 2 (April, 1970), and "Communal Discernment: Reflections on Experience," vol. IV, no. 5, (November 1972).

Luther and Ignatius lies in the latter's complementary Rules for Thinking with the Church [352-369].[6] He recognizes that the objective—the divine revelation given by God in its fullness through Jesus Christ and handed down through the living tradition of the Church—always controls the subjective—the individual's discernment of one's own spiritual experiences.[7] This insight of Ignatius goes back to the Letter to the Romans (c. 12), where St. Paul gives the principle that individual discernment—"the measure of faith that God has dealt to each of you" (v. 3)—must be exercised within and for the community: "so, all or us, united with Christ, form one body, serving individually as limbs and organs to one another" (v. 5). From this principle flowed the recognition from the beginning that the discernment of the individual is not fully confirmed by God, until it is confirmed by the Church community.

A way that can be helpful to the director, both for understanding the Rules for Discernment of Spirits and for explaining them to the retreatant, is to analyze them structurally. This reveals that they contain five basic considerations: (1) Description of the method of proceeding "characteristic of the evil spirit . . . and of the good spirit" [314], [315], [327]. (2) Description of the identifying marks of consolation and of desolation [316], [317]. (3) What one is to do when in desolation [318-320], [324, second paragraph], [325], [326]. (4) What are the principal causes of desolation [322]. (5) What one is to do when in consolation [323], [321, first paragraph].

It is notable that the largest number of rules have to do with what to do in desolation. This is understandable when one notes that the purpose of these rules for the First Week is to understand "the different movements produced in the soul and for recognizing those that are good, to admit them, and those

---

5.   See Leo Bakker, *Freiheit und Erfahrung* (Würzburg: Echter-Verlag, 1970).

6.   See the chapter "Rules for Thinking with the Church."

7.   Cf. Part I.

that are bad, to reject them" [313]. From experience Ignatius knew that a person in the First Week, coming to realization of the vision of the First Principle and Foundation and of its challenge to conversion, and reflecting on one's own inordinate affections and sinful actions, can often be tempted by the attractions of self-love or by the cost of discipleship. Thus, it is normal enough for the person to experience movements of desolation.[8]

This commentary will now follow these five basic considerations as they are developed in the Rules for the First Week.

First Consideration

Ignatius distinguishes the method of proceeding characteristic of evil spirits and of good spirits according to the basic orientation of a person. If this is away from God, then the force of evil is felt affectively through desires that move one toward actions contrary to the love of God and of other people, the consequence of centering oneself upon selfish self-love [314]. In a comparison drawn from his own experience as a soldier, Ignatius warns that the evil spirits will attack a person most tenaciously where that person is weakest [327]. Recognition of this fact of experience goes back in the tradition of Scripture (cf. Eph. 6:10-20), and is clearly developed by Antony of the Desert and all the following spiritual masters in the maxims of Christian asceticism. From this same tradition, Ignatius in the Exercises takes the powerful weapon of the daily particular examination of conscience to resist movements away from God where one finds self most vulnerable [21-31].

The Spirit of God works in a person through the light of reason, bringing to mind the law of love and its behavioral consequences illuminated by Christian conscience. Through the ex-

---

8. Ignatius is very insistent that the Rules for Discernment of Spirits II, for the Second Week [328336] not be presented to a retreatant until the signs are clear that one is ready for them. To present these prematurely would be "harmful" [9]. I present a commentary on these in the next chapter.

perience of these interior movements, a person can recognize experientially what is at present one's basic orientation, and with the help of the director can open self to the grace of conversion [314]; cf. [349].

If a person's basic orientation is toward God, the force of the evil spirit is felt through both affectivity and false reasons that bring lack of peace. In such a person the Spirit of God works through affectivity, bringing strength and joy and peace for living love [315].

The immediate object of spiritual discernment is *interior movements.* The traditional maxim for accurate discernment, "By their fruits you shall know them," refers to interior fruits before it refers to external good or bad actions.[9] The goal of this discernment of interior movements is to discover their *origin.* The means to identify the origin is to detect their *orientation:* are they moving one toward God or away from God? Do they lead to the profound experience of interior peace at the bottom of the heart or to disturbance there? A director must take note that the very possibility for a retreatant to do spiritual discernment demands that the person be in touch with his or her own feelings. If a person has been acculturated to suppress feelings, the first step in helping one to do spiritual discernment must be to help that person to become aware of one's own feelings, which may take a long time.

This method of discerning the origin of interior movements can be traced from Ignatius back through the entire tradition, through Cassian (360-430 A.D.) and Evagrius of Pontus (346-399 A.D.)—whom Cassian translated "after his fashion"—and the *Life of Antony,* written by St. Athanasius (c. 360), to the first developed doctrine of discernment of spirits given by Origen (185-254 A.D.). Basing himself on the Scriptural tradition and the practical advice of the Shepherd of Hermas, Origen points out that evil spirits and good spirits move persons "*in principale cordis nostrae,*" at the bottom of the heart. There are, then, three

---

9. Cf. Gal. 5:16-25.

sources of interior movements; (1) evil spirits, (2) good spirits. and (3) our own human reality. The problem of spiritual discernment is to recognize the origin of these movements. "for recognizing those that are good, to admit them, and those that are bad. to reject them" [313]. The entire tradition teaches that our choices and actions presuppose discernment of the source of our desires.

In presenting these rules to a retreatant, a director may need to point out that the traditional language employed by Ignatius is rooted in the biblical cosmology of good and evil spirits. Contemporary retreatants may not be at home with this language and may prefer Jungian or Freudian or other psychological interpretations of the levels of interior experiences. The important thing is to recognize interior movements that have a passive quality, that seem to "invade" us, whether the interpretation of these experiences is based upon archetypes, or unconscious, or id, or what have you. Ignatius and the other masters of the tradition necessarily interpreted experience according to the categories of their own historical and cultural situation, but they were very much in touch with the reality of the experience. For example, Evagrius of Pontus was a master of experimental psychology, quite aware of what contemporary psychology calls the "subconscious," although he expresses his experience through a "demonology," This itself reflects the depth of his psychology. Demon or disturbed subconscious, the result is the same: turbulence and temptation. The crucial matter, through the discernment, is to recognize which of the interior movements orient one to God and which orient one away from God.[10]

---

10. Ignatius says that the function of the one directing the Exercises is "to aid the retreatant to discern the effects of the good spirit and of the evil spirit" (my translation). This is in the "Autograph Directory," written down by Polanco, Ignatius' secretary. *Directoria Exercitiorum Spiritualium, 1540-1599*, (Rome: Historical Institute of the Society of Jesus, 1955), #19, p. 76.

Second Consideration

The director must possess a clear understanding of the distinguishing marks of consolation and desolation in order to help the retreatant do spiritual discernment. The description given by Ignatius of spiritual consolation in number 316 is clear and concrete. It can be developed a bit by noting remarks that Ignatius makes in the "Autograph Directory." He says that "the director should explain at length what consolation is, going through all the elements, such as: interior peace, spiritual joy, hope, faith, love, tears, and lifting of the mind—all of which are gifts of the Holy Spirit."[11] Further on, he lists "spiritual happiness, love, hope in the things from on high, tears, and every interior movement that leaves the soul consoled in the Lord."[12]

A director must carefully help the retreatant through reflection on experience to be able to distinguish the *levels* of interior feelings, in order to be able to differentiate merely sensible consolation or pious thoughts on more superficial levels of one's multidimensional self-awareness from the profound insight and deep love and joy and peace in the depths of one's spirit—at the bottom of the heart—which is true spiritual consolation.

In number 317 Ignatius provides a helpful description of spiritual desolation, also developed by him in the "Autograph Directory." "Desolation is the contrary (of consolation), from the evil spirit and the evil spirit's gifts, such as war against peace, sadness against spiritual joy, hope in base things against hope in high things, also low love against high love, dryness against tears, wandering of the mind in base things against lifting up of the mind."[13] Again, "The contrary of consolation is desolation: sadness, lack of trust, unlove, aridity, etc."[14]

---

11. *Ibid.*, #11, p. 72.

12. *Ibid.*, #18, p. 76.

13. *Ibid.*, #12, p. 72.

14. *Ibid.*, #8, p. 76.

Ignatius notes that "just as consolation is the opposite of desolation, so the thoughts that spring from consolation are the opposite of those that spring from desolation" [314]. Here, he again shows his continuity with the tradition of spiritual discernment. Origen, out of his Stoic philosophy, spoke of interior movements as "thoughts" that move us toward actions. Antony of the Desert saw the devil's weapon as an immense dust storm of "evil thoughts" to move us away from the way of light. Evagrius of Pontus, a much more subtle psychologist, developed the relation between sense and appetite, bodily motions, temperament, memory, and passions as sources of thoughts. Where Antony had mixed passions and thoughts, Evagrius clearly distinguished them. The senses, receiving impressions from external things, excite the passions from which arise the thoughts: interior movements away from God. Here Ignatius is warning us to recognize by their orientation the movements that are thoughts arising from spiritual desolation.

Third Consideration

Ignatius devotes most of his rules for the First Week to presenting a strategy for what to do when one is in desolation. This clearly reveals the pedagogical function of these rules. Mastering them through reflection on experience, with the help of the director, will enable the exercitant accurately to recognize true spiritual consolation or desolation at the bottom of the heart and to develop the ability to distinguish the movements toward God and away from God and, especially at this stage of the dynamic movement of the Exercises, to learn how to resist desolation and to grow spiritually through this very struggle. This experiential pedagogy prepares the retreatant to be able, when the time comes, to approach the election [175], [176] through the use of the more subtle Rules for the Discernment of Spirits of the Second Week [328-336].[15]

The most fundamental warning to a person experiencing desolation is never to make a decision while in this condition [318]. One can find God in peace (cf. [150]) only when, at the bottom of the heart, the presence of the Spirit of God is experienced, even if there is pain and repugnance at less profound levels of one's multidimensional self-awareness. When a person is in desolation, "guidance" through interior movements comes from evil spirits—the absence of God—and choices cannot be responses to the Holy Spirit. Thus, affectivity rooted in faith must enable the will of the exercitant to hold to decisions made during consolation, even when false rationalizations move one to change these.[16] Thus, if the retreatant is in desolation, the director must insist that no decisions be made until one has returned to spiritual consolation at the bottom of the heart.

With the entire tradition, Ignatius urges the person in desolation to struggle actively against it [319]. Again, the call is to the will, that is, affectivity, to take practical measures to open oneself to the gift of consolation. This call to active combat against desolation goes back to Scripture and is taken up by the Shepherd of Hermas, who sees the spiritual life as a fight against the demons. They are ejected by baptism, but they may come again to one who allows self to be won over by their suggestions. So, a person must strive against them, and the weapons of the struggle are prayer and fasting, which are seen to have the force of an exorcism. Antony of the Desert sees this spiritual combat waged through the ascetical practices of fasting and vigils undertaken by the Christian "hero" who has gone to the desert to engage in direct battle with the forces of evil. This image continues throughout the tradition and is taken up again by Ignatius.

---

15. See next chapter.
16. Cf. [315].

The person in desolation should call upon reason to reflect that the very desolation is allowed by God as a "testing" that will aid spiritual growth.[17] One must call upon faith to believe that, although not "felt" at a superficial level, the grace of God remains active at the bottom of the heart, so that one can endure [320]. Thus, one must patiently continue to move toward God by following the decisions made during consolation [321], cf. [319].

Ignatius calls the person to hold to faith that consolation will return. This is his way of invoking the traditional maxim, "when in desolation, remember consolation." Having been to the mountain before, even though now in darkness and desert, a person, by remembering the time on the mountain can vivify hope that God will take one there again in God's own good time. Thus, the director should encourage this perseverance and hope in a retreatant in desolation [7]. The director should help the person to remember that the grace of Jesus Christ, if one opens self to it, is always enough to resist movements away from God. By holding firmly to the Lord, one will always have sufficient strength [334]. Here again, Ignatius takes up the living tradition coming from Scripture to his own day. The Shepherd of Hermas had insisted that there is no need to be afraid of the devil, since the devil has no power against true faith. The devil has been overcome by Jesus Christ. Antony of the Desert pointed out that what the devil fears most in "ascetics" is their loyalty to Jesus Christ, and advised that if we wish to despise the enemy, we should always keep our thoughts on the things of the Lord.[18]

Using a metaphor that contemporary ears hear as "sexist" but which, actually, must reflect Ignatius' own experience as a

---

17. Cf. Therrien, *Le Discernement,* pp. 10-26, for an excellent treatment of the biblical notion of God testing persons to purify them in order the more fully to dwell within them.

18. After Ignatius, the great Jesuit mystic, St. Alphonsus Rodriguez, in the profundity of his simplicity, would recall this rule in the words, "To an incertitude that weakens, oppose a certitude that gives peace."

courtier with the ladies of his time, he points out that resistance to the movements away from God must be bold and must go directly against what the movements suggest [325]; fear is diabolical, so under attack a person must react with all one's strength, hoping in the Lord. Ignatius invokes here the basic ascetical principle of *agere contra* (cf. [16], [157], [350]).

As a balance to the preceding feminine metaphor, Ignatius offers the image of a "false lover" to make the point that in experiencing movements against going to God one must be totally open to one's spiritual director [326]. Here again, he is in continuity with the tradition. Antony of the Desert insisted that the *only* way to grow in discernment is through spiritual experience. In order to advance in ability to discern spirits, one must grow in clarity within one's own spirit. It is indispensable, therefore, that beginners manifest their most intimate thoughts to their spiritual director, so that in virtue of the director's experience, he or she may gradually communicate to the directee the ability to discern. It is for this reason that Ignatius sees the total openness of the exercitant to the director as the condition for direction of the Exercises [17].

Fourth Consideration

To enable the retreatant to know what one should do when in desolation, it is important that the director can help the person recognize the cause of any desolation. In number 322 Ignatius enumerates three principle causes: (1) "one's own fault"; (2) "testing" by God;[19] (3) passive purification by God. The first is discovered through examination of one's own active response to God and detection of ways that one is resisting grace or at least not cooperating with it; the response will be actively to cooperate with grace and to resist movements against it (cf. [12], [13], [16], [319], [320]). When one

---

19. See note 17, above.

finds no fault in his or her own efforts, the second is recognized by the experience that God is educating a person not to seek God for oneself rather than for Godself. This might be parallel to the "night of the senses" of John of the Cross. The response will be to persevere in one's efforts, trusting that consolation will be given again, after the period of testing (cf. [320], :321], [324]). The third is known by the quality of insight and the depth of experience of the desolation that brings one to surrender to a hollowing out by the Lord bringing one to the depth of spiritual poverty necessary to surrender totally to the gratuity of divine love. This might be parallel to the "night of the spirit" of John of the Cross. The response will be the same as to the second desolation.

Ignatius continues to reflect the tradition. Perhaps the most remarkable similarity of presentation of the doctrine of spiritual discernment to that of Ignatius by an early master of Christian spirituality is that given by Diadochus of Photice (c. 400-486 A.D.).[20] Diadochus speaks of desolation as the "retreat of God," and sees it as the result of a divine permission given to the devil to attack the spirit of the elect, as happened to Job. Every "retreat of God," indeed, delivers over the spirit to the attacks of Satan. Diadochus identifies two desolations:

1. *Educative desolation.* This is related to the biblical "testing" of the just. God manifests Godself to a person in the

---

20. Diadochus was a bishop who earlier was probably a monk and spiritual director of a monastery. He was ordained a lector by St. Basil and a deacon by St. Gregory Nazianzus. Through them he came to know the thought of Clement of Alexandria and Origen. Beginning as a disciple of St. Macarius, Diadochus lived for twenty-seven years in the Egyptian desert, and he combines the theology of the Cappadocians with the teaching of the Desert Fathers. He gives a marvelous distillation of the tradition of spiritual discernment in his major work, *One Hundred Chapters on Spiritual Perfection,* variously titled in different editions as, *On Gnostics* or *Practical Chapters on the Science of Spiritual Discernment,* with the subtitles "Spiritual Guide" or "Way of Perfection." Of particular note in tracing the tradition as it appears in Ignatius are chapters 26-35 and 75-89.

measure that one progresses in living love. Nevertheless, God also permits the person to experience being sought after by demons, in order that one may learn the discernment of good and evil spirits and become more humble. However, educative desolation does not in any way deprive the spirit of the divine light. It simply incites a person to seek, with profound humility, the help of God.[21]

2. *Desolation of dereliction.* This is the desolation experienced by a person who refuses to possess God. Nothing is lost if through this experience the person is moved to confess one's sins with tears.

The first principal reason for desolation given by Ignatius, then, corresponds to the "desolation of dereliction" and the second and the third to the "educative desolation." Recognizing the cause of the desolation through helping the retreatant to reflect upon one's experience, the director will be able to help the person to respond in the appropriate manner.

Fifth Consideration

Ignatius completes his rules for Discernment of Spirits for the First Week by indicating briefly what to do when in consolation. Picking up the traditional maxim, "When in consolation, remember desolation," he advises the person to reflect on future desolation and how to face it, when it comes, out of the lights

---

21. In the eighty-fifth of the *One Hundred Chapters,* Diadochus, speaking of persons far advanced in spiritual growth, teaches: "Even one who has reached this degree, God sometimes abandons to the malice of the demons, leaving one's intellect without light, in order that our liberty be not entirely chained by the bonds of grace, not only because these are struggles which triumph over sin, but also because the person should still make progress in spiritual experience. Because what one considers the perfection of the disciple is still imperfect before the richness of God, who teaches us with an ambitious love, even if one has succeeded, thanks to progress in works, to go up the entire ladder which was shown to Jacob (Gen. 28:12)."

and gifted strength now given [323]. Further, one must remind oneself that consolation is a gift from God and humbly accept it, while remembering from past experience how much one has depended upon it and, so, been incapacitated when deprived of it during times of desolation. The director will help the exercitant to follow this advice during times of consolation.

In summary, then, the director will present the Rules for Discernment of Spirits for the First Week when movements within the directee show that it is time to do this. Whether or not a director chooses to give the text of the Rules to the retreatant, it will be necessary to help the person to bring one's own feelings to conscious awareness, in order to discern them and to distinguish different levels of feelings, and so to be able to recognize by reflection on experience movements at the bottom of the heart. Through this reflection the retreatant must be helped to discern the origin of these movements by detecting their orientation—toward God or away from God. The director will assist the retreatant to know what to do when in desolation and when in consolation. Through this ongoing pedagogy, the retreatant will grow toward ability to use the Rules for Discernment of Spirits of the Second Week, commented upon in the next chapter.

Rules for Discernment of Spirits II [328-336]

The second set of Rules for Discernment of Spirits given by Ignatius in the *Spiritual Exercises* "serve for a more accurate discernment of spirits and are more suitable for the second week" [328]. In number 10 of the Introductory Observations, Ignatius tells the director that the proper time to explain these rules is "when the one who is giving the Exercises perceives that the exercitant is being assailed and tempted under the appearance of good," normally during the illuminative way, which corresponds to the exercises of the Second Week. A helpful way to understand these rules for explaining them to the retreatant is for the director to notice that structurally they offer three basic considerations: (1) Description of the manner of proceeding characteristic of good and evil spirits [329], [331], [332]. (2) How to discern the origin of a *caused* consolation as being from good or evil spirits by detecting its orientation [333-334], [336: last three sentences]. (3) The way to recognize when a consolation is without any doubt from God, and the need to distinguish the actual consolation from its "afterglow" [330], [336: first three sentences].

These rules are in clear continuity with the tradition of spiritual discernment from the beginning. The commentary will follow these three basic considerations.

First Consideration

Ignatius sums up the entire tradition of discernment, beginning with Scripture, by pointing out that it is characteristic of the Spirit of God to give consolation to the human spirit: "true happiness and spiritual joy," casting out sadness and turmoil brought about by the force of evil. Thus, it is through affectivity that the Holy Spirit acts at the bottom of the heart to draw one to God. However by working through false reasons, the force of evil tries to cast out this consolation [329], cf. [316], [317]. Thus, when the basic orientation of a person is toward God, the evil one may masquerade as an angel of light, giving consolation in order eventually to draw the person away from God [331], [332].[22]

---

22. Ignatius here reflects the experience of centuries of Christian struggle to grow in the Lord. Diadochus of Photice (see preceding chapter with note 20) develops the "two consolations" in chapter 30-33 of the *One Hundred Chapters*: "When our intellect begins to experience the consolation of the Holy Spirit, then Satan also consoles the soul by a feeling of false sweetness" (ch. 31); "The first kind (of consolation) indeed, as soon as it comes from God, ordinarily invites the souls of the athletes (Diadochus's word for a Christian striving for spiritual progress) of devotion to love within a great outpouring of the soul; the other kind, which normally agitates the soul under a wind of illusion, tries . . . to conceal the meaning of its experience from the intellect that retains intact the remembering of God" (ch. 32).

As an example, one may be moved to call his or her community to greater authenticity in Christian living, such as through
stricter poverty, and end in bitterness or schism; or, moved to
speak prophetically and end as a Pharisee; or moved to a life of
intense prayer and end in pride. What began as a good ends in evil
and prepares for a gradually increasing movement away from God
[331]. The crux of the matter, then, to discern the origin of the
consolation, is to detect its orientation: does it draw one toward
God or away from God? A consolation that moves one more toward God can only come from the spirit of God.[23] A consolation,
however good its apparent orientation in the beginning, that at last
leads us away from God is from the evil one.

Second Consideration

Thus, Ignatius points out, we must reflect carefully on the
whole progression of our thoughts: how they begin, how they proceed, and where they finally lead us. When the entire progression
of thoughts has moved us toward God, we know that the consolation was from the Spirit of God; on the other hand, when gradually
as the thoughts progress, or when clearly at the end to which they
move us, we find that we have been moving away from God, it is
evident that the consolation came from the evil one.

Ignatius gives examples of change of affectivity: the "peace,
tranquility, and quiet" of the initial consolation give way to dis-
quiet and disturbance at the bottom of the heart [333]. This touchstone for detecting the origin of movements through their orienta-

---

23. Cf. St. Augustine: It is not to receive a thing; it is to receive true love. It
is to receive this movement by which God communicates divine life to
persons, the accumulation of God's gifts. One can move toward God only in
taking up again the movement of love which has brought God to come toward
us. *Tractatus in Epistolam Joannis ad Parthos,* ed. Paul Agaesse, S.J. (Paris:
Cerf, 1961) pp. 96-97. This commentary on the First Epistle of John is one of
the great documents in the tradition of spiritual discernment.

tion is explicit from the beginning of the tradition of spiritual discernment; for example, "By their fruit you shall know them."

The Shepherd of Hermas in the Sixth Mandatum gives a very concrete description of this discernment procedure, to which Ignatius is completely true:

> How, then . . . shall I know their workings, seeing that both angels dwell in me? Hear, saith he, the angel of righteousness is delicate and bashful and gentle and tranquil. When then this one enters the heart, forthwith he speaketh to thee of righteousness, of purity, of holiness, and of contentment, of every righteous deed. . . . When all these things enter into the heart, know that the angel of righteousness is with thee. Now see the works of the angel of wickedness also. First of all, he is quicktempered and bitter and senseless, and his works are evil, overthrowing the servants of God . . . Whenever a fit of angry temper or bitterness comes upon thee, know that he is in thee. (2:2-5)

In the Life of Antony (cc. 22-38, especially cc. 35-36), the effort is made to draw up rules for discerning spirits by contrasting their effects within the human spirit:

1. Good spirits are not turbulent, but come so quietly that, instantly, joy and gladness and courage arise in the soul, and the thoughts of the soul remain untroubled and unruffled. A longing for divine things and for things of the future life takes possession of the soul. Its joy and its tranquility betoken the holiness of the one who is present.

2. Evil spirits are full of confusion and come crashing, roaring, shouting. This at once begets terror in the soul, disturbance, disorder, and confusion of thoughts. This can lead to dejection, hatred of ascetics, indifference, and, finally, a desire for evil and a complete subversion of character. It is enemies that are present.[24]

---

24. L. Lorie, S.J., *Spiritual Terminology in the Latin Translation of the Vita Antonii with Reference to 4th and 5th Century Monastic Literature* (Nijmegen: Dekker & van de Vegt, N.V. 1955).

In order to clarify discernment of the origin of a caused consolation, Ignatius starts with a consideration of the *end* of the progression of thoughts in number 333, then draws attention in number 334 to the *middle*—the progressive movement from *beginning* to end, and, finally, in number 335 comes back to the beginning of this progression. Through an ending that has drawn me from God, we know that what seemed good at the beginning actually was from the evil one, and so by reflection on the middle a person can learn from experience how to better practice in the future the art of discernment of spirits [334]. The director can help the exercitant learn to be a discerning person through calling one to this reflection.[25] Diadochus of Photice had put it: "It is necessary to discern the suggestions that *run through* the mind, and to deposit in the treasures of the memory those which are good and come from God, while rejecting those which are perverse and diabolical."[26] This growth in ability to discern spirits is vital for continuing growth in holiness, for, as Antony of the Desert had pointed out, "the ascetic becomes more conscious of the working of good and evil spirits according as one rises to higher degrees of perfection."[27]

Returning to the beginning of the progression of thoughts—the origin of the movement discovered by detecting its orientation—Ignatius recalls that the action of good and evil spirits within the human spirit is felt according to the basic orientation of a person: toward God or away from God [335], cf. [314], [315]. If the orientation is toward God, Ignatius explains in number 335 that the action of the good spirit is experienced

---

25. Ignatius remarks, "Moving through the meditations on Christ our Lord, one reflects, when in consolation, upon the direction in which the Lord moves one, and in the same way, when one is in desolation" (my translation and underlined words). This is in the "Autograph Directory," *Directoria Exercitiorum Spiritualium, 1540-1599* (Rome: Historical Institute of the Society of Jesus, 1955), #18, p. 76.

26. *One Hundred Chapters*, ch. 26 (my emphasis).

27. Lorie, *Spiritual Terminology*, p. 107.

affectively as delicate and gentle and delightful, like "a drop of water penetrating a sponge"; the action of the evil spirit is experienced affectively by such a person as "violent, noisy, and disturbing . . . like a drop of water falling on a stone."[28] If the basic orientation of the person is away from God, the affective experiences at the bottom of the heart are just the opposite. In either case, the basic orientation of the person will determine whether good or evil spirits are experienced as entering "with noise and commotion" since they are contrary to this orientation, or "silently" since they are in accord with it.[29] If one is to be capable of doing this discernment of spirits, the director must have led the person through the pedagogy of the Rules for Discernment of the First Week [317-327], helping the individual to be in touch with his or her own feelings and to distinguish their level within one's multidimensional self-awareness.[30]

Third Consideration

The need for actually doing discernment of spirits arises when a consolation is *caused*. However, when one experiences consolation "without any previous cause" [330], there is no need to discern its origin, because "there can be no deception in it, since it can proceed from God our Lord only" [336]. Ignatius explains that by a consolation without any previous cause, he means an affective experience at the bottom of the heart that has no proportionate cause in perception or knowledge. It is not a matter, therefore, of suddenly experiencing consolation, but rather, perhaps after an extended period of prayer and asceticism, being gifted with a depth of consolation beyond the capability of these efforts to produce. It is the affective experience at

---

28. Cf. the Shepherd of Hermas and Antony of the Desert, discussed previously.

29. See the preceding chapter.

30. See the preceding chapter.

the bottom of the heart of *being drawn wholly* to the love of God. This consolation, then, is characterized by the experience of *passivity* and *gratuity*. "It belongs solely to the Creator to come into a soul, to leave it, to act upon it, to draw it wholly . . ." [330].[31]

Hence, the director must help the retreatant through reflection on experience to identify the quality of experience at the bottom of the heart and to be able to recognize the passivity and gratuity of consolation felt there. It can be useful for the director, and possibly an aid to some retreatants, to have a particular philosophical interpretation of the experience of consolation without previous cause.[32] But the important thing is to help the exercitant to get in touch with the experience and to be able to distinguish it from any other experience through means of reflecting on experience.[33] It is absolutely crucial (there is no other way!) that the person know *by experience* when a consolation is certainly from the Lord and can be from no other. For example, the entire tradition identifies peace as one of the certain signs of the presence of the Lord. But unless a person by reflection on experience can distinguish the unique peace at the bottom of the heart—which without possibility of doubt indicates the presence of God—from more superficial levels of peace—brought for example, from "I got what I wanted," or from "What a relief to have made a decision and no longer to be in anxious tension waiting to make a choice"—then, one is always open to illusion.[34] Through reflection on experience, a person can come to recognize the unique peace

---

31. Cf. Diadochus of Photice: "Grace has pitched its tent in the *core of the soul*, while the evil spirits sojourn around the members of the heart" (my emphasis). *One Hundred Chapters*, ch. 33.

32. For useful contemporary philosophical interpretations, see Karl Rahner, S.J., *The Dynamic Element in the Church* (New York: Herder and Herder, 1964), and Daniel Gil, S.J., *La Consolacion sin cause precedente* (Rome: C.I.S., 1971).

33. A practical help here can be the exercise in "dynamic memory," explained in Appendix I.

34. See preceding chapter.

which is always *gifted*, always *passive*, always a *certain* sign
that "It is the Lord!"

There are two characteristics of this unique consolation:

1. The person knows by experience that it is impossible at will
   to bring about this consolation at the bottom of the heart
   through any technique or intentional activity. One can prepare oneself for this gift and wait for it, but never cause it.
   It is always experienced, when it comes, as *gratuitous*.

2. The experience is always that of a *presence*, mysterious, but
   real; immanent and transcendent at once. One is aware at the
   very quick of one's existence of a completion, of "coming
   home," in the experience of the presence of Another, who
   cannot be contained in any concept or thought or image, who
   is at once here and beyond, and who is named only by faith in
   God's revelation to us in Jesus Christ.

Ignatius writes from his own experience, but he reflects the
entire tradition of spiritual discernment beginning in Scripture.
The consolation without previous cause is the Holy Spirit present within us actuating its presence and power to enable us affectively to experience God's presence.[35] If we trace this faith
insight from Scripture through the tradition, we find many out-
standing expressions of it. Origen identifies the place of the
Spirit within us as the bottom of our heart—"*in principale cordis nostrae*"—beyond reason, the irascible, and concupiscence.
Antony of the Desert locates it in the core of our spirit—"*to
noeron tes psyches*"—where God is present within us, the "still
point." When this core is perfectly free to *be* we have come to
perfection, and the peace of this core is the *touchstone* by which

---

35. Some New Testament texts that underlie the recognition of this experience
are: John 14:16-17, 26-27; Rom. 5:5, 8:14-16; 1 Cor. 2:10-16; 2 Cor. 1:21-22,
4:6, 13:5; Gal. 5:22-23; Eph. 1:14, 17-19, 3:16-19, 4:30; Phil. 2:1, 4:7, 9-10;
Col. 3:10, 15; 2 Thess. 3:5, 16; 2 Tim. 1:7; Titus 3:6-7; Heb. 4:14, 11:1,
13:21; 1 John 14:16-17, 26-27, 3:19-24, 4:4, 13, 5:9-10; James 3-:17-18; 1
Pet. 3:15; 2 Pet. 1:3, 10.

inward movements are to be tested to discern their origin.[36] For Cassian, this place is the *conscience,* which he defines as the "transparence of the spirit of God," which conditions the exercise of discernment. St. John Climacus in the Ladder of Paradise, on the 29th step, describes this place, reached by *apatheia,* as the center where one possessed God, who living in one, governs thoughts, words, and actions. Here, God interiorly illuminates one, makes one know the divine will, and acts in one. In a word, it is no longer the person who lives, but it is Christ who lives in one. For St. Augustine, it is a *root* in our spirits, where the unction of the Holy Spirit is active, where God gives testimony within us, a testimony which is *certain,* because it gives its own light.[37]

Diadochus of Photice, in the thirty-third of the *One Hundred Chapters,* wrote, "If by a movement which is unmistakable and free from any imagination, the soul is inflamed with love for God, as if it were drawing the body itself into the depths of this ineffable love . . . undergoing the influence of divine grace; when the soul no longer conceives anything at all of that toward which it is moved, then it is certain that this is the action of the Holy Spirit. Because entirely penetrated by this unspeakable sweetness, it can no longer think of anything else, since an unadulterated joy transports it." St. Bernard put it, "Constantly listen to what the Lord says within you, for what God says is peace." Meister Eckhart (1260-1328) located the primordial experience of the presence of God in the "spark of the soul" (*scintilla animae*). This is the source of discernment, because it is the experience that enables one to reject what draws the soul out of itself—away from God—and of knowing how to follow what draws the soul to its own true self: pure responsiveness to God. "The spark of the soul, which is created by God, is a light pressed in from above. It is the image of the divine nature, and

---

36. Lorie, *Spiritual Terminology,* p. 111.
37. *Op. cit.,* p. 85. Cf. Treatise III, 12.

it is always turned toward the good. . . . It has two works. First, it is the bit against that which is not pure. Its second work is that it always attracts to the good."[38] Consolation without previous cause is an experience of God, present always in the *scintilla animae*, God's presence affectively felt by a person.[39]

Thomas a Kempis eloquently sums up the approach of the "devotio moderna" to the experience of consolation without previous cause: "O Liqht unending, O Light surpassing all that shines in your creation; send down from on high the lightning stroke of your dazzling brilliance to pierce and free from darkness the most secret depths of my heart. Seize my spirit and all its powers. Give it your purity, your gladness, your brightness, your life; that it may cling to you in an ecstasy of joy . . . that longed-for hour, when the joy of your presence shall brim to overflowing the depths of my desire, and you be my all in all!" (III.24). While it is likely that Ignatius never read any of these citations other than that from the *Imitation of Christ,* it is clear that from reflection on his own experience, his doctrine on consolation without previous cause is in continuity with the whole tradition of spiritual discernment.

---

38. Sermon, "Homo Quidam Fecit Cenam Magnam," J.M. Clark, *Meister Eckhart: An Introduction and Anthology* (London: 1957), pp. 158-160.

39. The Rheno-Flemish mystics were highly intellectual in their approach to the spiritual life. Eckart's notion of the *scintilla animae* came to him by way of the doctrine of Albert the Great on the "agent intellect." For Albert, basically a Platonist, the agent intellect is a part of the highly structured soul, a part directly illuminated by the divine light. The immediate predecessor of Eckhart was Thierry of Freiberg, who was a student of Albert. For Thierry, the agent intellect works in the *abditum nentis*—the profoundest depths of the memory. It is like a sea of intellectuality, the mark which God has imprinted on human persons to make his image shine there. By this supreme character the substance of the soul becomes *deiform* and is inserted into eternity. Essentially, it is a pure and simple intelligence that proceeds from God and never ceases to turn itself toward God, so that the emanation is not distinguished from its return to its source. Thus, God is within the most profound depth of the soul, where God is more present than we are to ourselves.

Although the experience of consolation without previous cause requires no discernment, because "there can be no deception in it" [336], Ignatius warns of the necessity to carefully distinguish the "afterglow" from the actual consolation. The enduring joy of such a consolation, often permeating many of the multidimensional levels of self-awareness, can last a long time, even days. By reflecting on the qualities of affective experience, one must be able to distinguish the time of the actual consolation without cause from the time thereafter when one is still sensibly consoled, during which time one's own reason can interject concepts and judgments not immediately from God. Thus, one can fall into the illusion of thinking that "God told me to do this," when, actually one told oneself to do it. Having distinguished these moments, one must then discern the subsequent judgments according to the usual rules for discernment of spirits: discovering the origin of these thoughts by detecting their orientation [333-335]. With the entire tradition, Ignatius recognizes that their origin may be: (1) good spirits; (2) evil spirits; or (3) one's own human reality through one's own concepts and judgments.[40] The director must help the retreatant through reflection upon experience to be able to distinguish the afterglow from the consolation without previous cause and to discern the origin of the movements experienced during the afterglow.

Basis for Finding God in All Things

The rules given by Ignatius, drawn from the tradition, are intended to help the retreatant to do *discernment of spirits,* that is, to discover the origin of interior movements by detecting their orientation. The entire dynamic movement of the Spiritual Exercises has as its goal the day by day living-out of discerned responses to the actual Word of God here and now—finding God in all things. The application of the discernment of spirits

---

40. Cf. the preceding chapter; also cf, [32].

to choice and action through following out in behavior the movement discerned to originate from the Holy Spirit is made explicitly by Ignatius in the first and second times of election [175], [176].[41] The ordering of discernment of spirits to *total* discernment to see and choose and do what God calls one to here and now is evident in the tradition from the beginning, although it becomes clearly articulated first of all in the writings of Evagrius of Pontus.[42]

The Shepherd of Hermas was concerned, through discernment of Spirits, to help the disciple to practice virtue and to avoid vice. Origen developed discernment of spirits to its termination in a moral judgment, although he does not extend discernment to the actual execution of the choice. His whole purpose, however, was to help people to live holiness. Antony of the Desert saw discernment of spirits as the necessary means for the monk to live a perfect Christian life.[43] Evagrius of pontus taught that through accurate discernment of spirits, a person could choose to follow thoughts that guard the measure in actions—the right middle way—fitting Christian actions to the actual situation here and now. Evagrius, thus, extended the meaning of the word "discernment" beyond that of the first, essential step of discernment of spirits to the *total* discernment that terminates in the right Christian behavior. Cassian, in taking up this tradition, extended the discernment to actions in their least details. For him, discernment in its full meaning is more or less identified with moderation. The origin of movements from the evil one is revealed by their orientation to immoderate actions to which they impel us. Moderated actions are the result of discern-

---

41. See "Dynamics of the Second Week," in Part II.

42. See my study "Ignatian Discernment," *Studies in the Spirituality of Jesuits*, vol. II, no. 2 (April, 1970) pp. 47-48. For historical development, see the work of Fr. Dingjan, O.S.B. *Discretio: les origines patristiques et monastiques de la doctrine sur la prudence chez Saint Thomas d'Aquin* (Assen: Van Gorcum & Co., N.V., 1967).

43. Lorie, *Spiritual Terminology,* p. 107.

ment between what is excessive and vicious, and so from the evil one, from what is measured and virtuous and so from the Spirit of God. Discernment puts one on the *via regia*, the "royal way" of the golden mean. After Cassian, the tradition continues to present *total* discernment, of which discernment of spirits is the first necessary step.[44]

Constants of Spiritual Discernment

In summary, it is clear that it is the Scriptural vision of spiritual discernment that is passed down through the tradition to Ignatius. The constants of the tradition are:

1. The *immediate object* of discernment is interior impulses to action: passions, thoughts, feelings, motions.

2. The *goal* of discernment is to detect the origin of the impulses: which of these are from the Holy Spirit and which are not (*discernment of spirits*), in order to follow out in action the movement from the Holy Spirit (*total discernment*).

3. The *means* to achieve this goal is to discover the orientation of an impulse to action: is it, or is it not, leading one to an action in *harmony* with God's action in one's own life?

4. To discover this orientation, it is necessary to reflect upon three *givens:* (a) the authentic interpretation of *past* experience, both community and personal [45]; (b) the gathered evidence of present experience; (c) the already discerned *future* given by one's already discerned vocational call to be fulfilled in response to God until death. This begins with the primordial discernment of the origin of Jesus Christ from God, responded to through acceptance of the gift of faith.[46] It is further specified through discernment of the or-

---

44. Cf. Dingjan, *Discretio.*

45. See the following chapter on "Rules for Thinking with the Church."

46. Cf. my "Ignatian Discernment," *Studies,* pp. 73-74.

igin of the Church from Jesus, responded to through baptism. Further identification is given through discernment of the call to a Christian vocation to which one is moved by the Holy Spirit, responded to as lay person or religious or priest. Depending upon how far one has already progressed in this series of "identification" discernments, an election will look to whichever one follows. Finally, the discernment will concern how to live out this vocation in daily behavior most authentically.

It is by finding the harmony among these three givens that a person is able to experience the unique peace that confirms with certitude that one has found God, responding to His actual word to one here and now through choice and action. Discernment, then, is the result of a graced effort at *interior liberation,* leading to *encounter with God* and to a fully free *personal choice,* which is a personal response to a personal call from God. To live discernment is to find God in all things. This is the goal of the entire dynamic movement of the Spiritual Exercises. The role of the director is to help the exercitant to attain this goal.[47]

Rules for Thinking with the Church [352-370]

Ignatius' Rules for Thinking with the Church are an integral element within the dynamic movement of the Spiritual Exercises, both because of the expression of the deep faith in and love of the real, human community of the Church to which the entire movement of the Exercises impels the exercitant,[48] and because of their crucial importance as the criterion of individual discernment.[49] Whether or not the director chooses to present the text of the rules to a retreatant, it is nevertheless very im-

---

47. *Ibid.,* pp. 74-76.
48. See "Dynamics of the Fourth Week," in Part III.
49. See "Discernment of Spirits I," in Part III.

portant to help one to shape his or her attitude toward the Church according to the intention of these rules.[50]

For an understanding of this intention, it is helpful to analyze the rules into two basic considerations: (1) Insistence upon the need for a profound *affective attitude* of love for the Church, shaping an ecclesial mentality in response to issues facing the Church community [352], [353], [361], [362], [365]. (2) Examples of such issues during the historical time of Ignatius [354-360], [363], [364], [366], [370].

My commentary will follow the two basic considerations presented in these rules.

First Consideration

That the intention of Ignatius is to form a profound *affective attitude* shaping an ecclesial mentality is clear from his title for these rules and from the imagery that he uses in describing this attitude. The English translation, "Rules for Thinking with the Church," is misleading because of the intellectual connotation of "thinking," whereas Ignatius' own Spanish is "for the authentic *sentido* that we should have in the Church." *Sentido* is a form of the verb *sentir,* one of the key words, with its cognates, in the vocabulary of Ignatius.[51]

---

50. A very useful aid for the director's understanding of these rules is the Study "On Thinking with the Church Today," by John H. Wright, S.J., and Ladislas Orsy, S.J., *Studies in the Spirituality of Jesuits,* vol. VII, no. 1 (January, 1975). Cf. George E. Ganss, S.J., "Thinking with the Church: The Spirit of St. Ignatius' Rules," *The Way* Supplement 20 (Autumn, 1873), pp. 72-82.

51. See the analysis of Ignatian meanings of *sentir* in my *Making an Apostolic Community of Love* (St. Louis: The Institute of Jesuit Sources, 1970) pp. 111-116. For a list of all Ignatius' uses of the word and its cognates, see my "Vocabulary Tables," *Dossier "Constitutiones" A* (Rome: Centrum Ignatianum Spiritualitatis, 1972), pp. 149152. Cf. I. Iparraguirre, S.J., *Vocabulario de Ejercicios Espirituales: Ensayo de hermeneutica Ignaciana* (Rome: Centrum Ignatianum Spiritualitatis, 1972), pp. 192-197.

This word has many highly nuanced meanings in his total vocabulary. In the title of these rules, it has a meaning very frequent in many contexts: *felt-knowledge*—love-knowledge, a knowing with the heart.[52]

Authentic *sentido* refers to felt-knowledge based upon the affective resonance experienced when reflecting on ecclesial issues, a felt-knowledge of how to respond to these issues, which is rooted in one's basic existential attitude of love for the Church and the ruling desire to be in union with the Church. Thus, the authentic *sentido* is a way of existing, before it is a conscious judgement. It is a radical operational attitude, a "bent of being," a profound, dynamic orientation of the person toward God, incarnationally continuing through the human community of the Church the mission of Jesus Christ to bring the Kingdom to be.[53] This radical, affective attitude is shaped by a depth of

---

52. Many commentators, following especially H. Pinard de la Boullaye, S.J., have given overly intellectualistic interpretations of the meaning of *sentir* in the title of these rules and in other Ignatian contexts, which are inadequate in view of a detailed analysis of Ignatius' vocabulary, which reveals the remarkable concreteness of his consciousness. Knowing, for him, was not merely intellectual, but a total human experience suffused with affectivity. Perhaps the difficulty arises from using a rationalistic philosophical approach to interpretation of experience. I have found more helpful for my own understanding of the central role of affectivity and love-knowledge (*sentir*) in these rules and in the discernment process the works of such scholars as John Baillie, *The Sense of the Presence of God,* Gifford Lectures, 1961-62 (Oxford Press: 1962); and John E. Smith, *Experience and God* (New York: Oxford, 1968). C.G. Jung supports "felt-knowledge" by insisting that of the four functions of the psyche *feeling* should rank with *thinking* as rational, in contrast to the other two, sensation and intuition: "Feeling is a kind of judging, differing, however, from an intellectual judgement in that it does not aim at establishing an intellectual conviction, but is solely concerned with the setting up of a subjective criterion of acceptance or rejection. Feeling, like thinking, is a rational function, since, as is shown by experience, values in general are bestowed according to the laws of reason, just as concepts in general are framed after the laws of reason." *Psychological Types* (London: 1923), p. 543.

53. See "Dynamics of the Kingdom of Christ Meditation," in Part II.

personal love for the Church, grounded in faith, that will move a person to respond spontaneously in ways that guard and build up the unity of the Church. Judgement about issues that attack this unity will be guided by the vital testimony of the love-knowledge—the authentic *sentido*—always orienting one toward communion with the Church.[54]

Ignatius did not philosophize about felt-knowledge; he experienced it. His experience is in direct continuity with the tradition. Paul, in his Letter to the Philippians, prayed that "your *love* may grow ever richer in knowledge and insight of every kind, and may thus bring you the gift of true discernment" (1:9). For Augustine, love is the source of knowledge of God and the means of discernment.[55] The source of all is the love with which the Father has loved us, even when we were sinners, manifested in Jesus Christ. To recognize this love, to accept it, to allow oneself to be judged by it, to be saved by it is the faith itself which is much more than simple adhesion to revealed truths. To accept this love is to be seized by it, and to experience, imperfectly but really, the gratuity of divine love. Faith and love are two poles of one fundamental attitude: love-knowledge. This knowledge is not a "conclusion," but is experienced, seized as an interior presence, even though only faith allows us to give this Love its true name. Through this felt-knowledge of love, God is known not as an object of knowledge but as a subject more present to us than we are to ourselves. Augustine recognizes this as an evident, primordial experience beyond intellectual explanation. He identifies it as the invisible "unction of

---

54. The function of the affective attitude toward the Church, then, is akin to the function of affectivity in the discernment of spirits. Ignatius entitled those rules, "for in some way to *sentir* and understand the different movements" [313]. It is through affectivity that one successfully comes to understand the origin of interior movements. See the preceding chapter.

55. His doctrine is developed in the *Tractatus in Epistolam Joannis ad Parthos,* ed., Paul Agaesse, S.J. (Paris, Cerf, 1961), and rooted in the philosophy and theology of love given in the *De Trinitate* VIII and IX.

the Holy Spirit," God giving testimony within us, a testimony that is certain, because it gives its own light.[56]

Diadochus of Photice, in the thirtieth of the *One Hundred Chapters*, likens the felt-knowledge of the intellect to the infallibility of healthy bodily sense-experience.[57] William of St. Thierry speaks of "the sense of enlightened love," and of how "from here love itself is understanding." He advises "to know God by loving God," and God insists that, "love of God itself is knowledge of him; unless God is loved God is not known."[58] To understand the function of love-knowledge for discernment and for thinking with the Church in the work of St. Thomas Aquinas, it is necessary to go, not to his doctrine on discretion, which he has developed as the moral virtue of prudence,[59] but to his treatment of the experiential knowledge of the Divine Persons inhabiting the soul of the just person and of the gifts of the

---

56. *Ibid.,* pp. 30; 49; 50-51; 85; 86.

57. "The sense of the intellect is an exact taste for the things that one discerns. Indeed, in the same way that by our bodily sense of taste, when it works well, we discern without error the good from the bad, and we move toward what is sweet; so, in the same way, when our intellect begins to move itself in full health and great detachment, it can richly experience the divine consolation and never allow itself to be drawn by what is opposed to it. As the body, indeed, in relishing earthly sweetnesses is infallible through sense experience, so also when the intellect rejoices above the counsels of the flesh, it can relish without error the consolation of the Holy Spirit . . . and it can retain, by the action of love, an unforgettable memory of this taste, testing by it infallibly that which is best." (XXX)

58. William's underlying principle is that "the mind is the soul's internal sense faculty. Nevertheless, the noblest sense faculty, the keenest, most powerful intellect, appears to be love, on condition that it is pure, for it is by it, as by a sense faculty, that the Creator is perceived by the creature; it is that which, like an intellect, gives intelligence to God." *Rule and Life*, ed. by M. Basic Pennington, O.C.S.O. (Spencer, Mass., Cistercian Publications, 1971), p. 46.

59. Cf. Fr. Dingjan, O.S.B., *Discretio: les origines patristiques et monastiques de la doctrine sur la prudence chez saint Thomas d'Aquin* (Assen: Van Gorcum and Co., N.V., 1967).

Holy Spirit flowing from this inhabitation, especially the gift of Wisdom.[60] The *devotio moderna*, which influenced Ignatius through the *Imitation of Christ*, strongly stressed affectivity. Thus, Ignatius, reflecting on his own experience, simply continues the tradition in his notion of felt-knowledge.

Through the graces given to the retreatant during the contemplation of the mysteries of the life of Jesus, especially those of the Fourth Week, the director must help one to grow consciously in the ecclesial mentality flowing from the affective attitude of love of the Church. Today, in a time when carping criticism of the human Church and feelings of frustration with it or anger toward it are widespread, this may require a real turnaround of feelings and of mentality in some retreatants. An ecclesial mentality is one that tends spontaneously to seek publicly to defend the Church. Thus, Ignatius says that we should put aside personal judgments and hold ourselves (*animo*)[61] always ready to be entirely obedient to the

---

60. During the time of St. Thomas it was commonly taught at Paris that the knowledge necessary for the invisible mission of the Trinity within the human spirit must be more than mere informed faith. It must include a supernatural, spiritual *taste*. The Schoolmen often called this an affective or experimental knowledge—a "felt-knowledge" because it is linked to the affective experience of love and of spiritual delight. St. Thomas insisted that the just person's knowledge of the Divine Persons inhabiting one's spirit must be not solely informed faith but knowledge accompanied by love, that is to say, a felt-knowledge. He teaches that such knowledge belongs to wisdom: union with God through love, which provides the just person the basis for a just estimation of God and God's Creatures—the source of discernment. It is from this spiritual feeling that one learns to esteem correctly God and God's creatures. One learns divine things by experiencing them. Cf. John F. Dedek, *Experimental Knowledge of the Indwelling Trinity: An Historical Study of the Doctrine of St. Thomas* (Mundelein, Ill., 1958), especially pp. 146-148.

The tradition, as it has been handed down in Orthodoxy, is summarized by the great nineteenth century spiritual master, Theophane the Recluse. He insists that for real encounter with God, it is necessary that "the heart feels what the mind is thinking." *The Art of Prayer: An Orthodox Anthology,* Igumen Chariton of Valamo, trans. E. Kadloubovsky and E.M. Palmer (London and Boston: Faber and Faber, 1966), p. 67.

hierarchical Church [353]. The point of specifying the *hierarchical* Church is to emphasize the incarnational reality of the human community with its human authority structure to which we are called to give obedience. That this ecclesial mentality is rooted in love of the Church is shown by Ignatius seeing the Church as the "true Spouse of Christ, our holy Mother."[62]

A person with an ecclesial mentality will tend always to praise what the Church determines, holding oneself (*animo*) ready to seek reasons to support rather than to attack [361]. Ignatius develops this as a spontaneous readiness in favor of what persons having authority in the Church say and do as opposed to a spontaneous tendency to criticize them. By helping a person to get in touch with these tendencies, the director will assist a retreatant to test whether one truly has an ecclesial mentality. Ignatius was perfectly aware that Church authorities could, as a matter of fact, say and do things objectively blameworthy. He had ample experience of this in his own day! He insists nevertheless, that one with an ecclesial mentality will not publicly speak against them, since this would cause scandal or discontent among people, and therefore militate against order and unity within the Churcn community, as

---

61. The word *animo* in this rule is often translated as the "mind." But the Spanish word of Ignatius refers to the *whole person.* Cf. George E. Ganss, S.J., in his introduction to *The Constitutions of the Society of Jesus* (St. Louis: The Institute of Jesuit Sources, 1970), p. 77, note 10.

62. Cf. the study of George E. Ganss, S.J., "On Thinking with the Church Today," *Studies,* p. 19. He writes: "He (Ignatius) is writing the language, not of apologetics or of theology (though he draws from it), but of love. Any true man may well see human defects in his mother. But he loves her still and endeavors to help her, both by trying tactfully and respectfully to remedy the defects if possible, and by defending her against unreasonable, over-hasty, or captious criticism. So is it also in regard to the Church. But only one who in spite of them all still views her love as his Mother and the spouse of Christ is likely to grasp the spirit or tenor of thought running through all these Rules."

well as in civil society.[63] Ignatius had been deeply scandalized by the carping criticism and sarcastic wit of Erasmus, which seemed to him to be speaking evil of superiors in their absence, and doing great harm to the hearers. A contemporary exercitant can he helped to test one's own ecclesial mentality by reflecting upon one's spontaneous way of speaking about authorities in the Church. Public carping criticism or sarcastic wit show that one has not developed such a mentality. On the other hand, Ignatius' own experience and practice. even with respect to popes, are reflected in his realistic advice that efforts should be made to correct the bad conduct of superiors by taking effective means to do this.[64]

That this ecclesial mentality flowing from the affective attitude of deep love of the Church is grounded in faith is forcefully articulated by Ignatius when he says that even if something "seems to me white, I will believe black if the hierarchical Church so defines" (*determina*) [365]. The point of this strongly rhetorical thrust at Erasmus is that a true believer must hold defined mysteries on faith, even though their paradox confounds limited human understanding.[65] The Holy Spirit gifts a person with the faith to confess that "Jesus is Lord" (1 Cor.

---

63. The reference to "secular superiors" should not be read as a blind loyalty to absolute monarchs. Ignatius' whole notion of authority was rooted in the Castilian political philosophy that the power of rulers ultimately comes from the people and can be taken away by them. Cf. my *Making an Apostolic Community of Love*, pp. 62-64 ; 74 ; 84-95 ; 90, note 26.

64. Even in the case of popes, Ignatius followed the principles he developed for making representations to change the commands of superiors, when authentic discernment indicates the need to do this. Ibid., pp. 137-142.

65. As did Lefevre de 'Estaples, Erasmus blended with his humanism and evangelism a strong dose of criticism of the pope. This was as much a scandal to the Castilian sense of fealty of Ignatius as it was a shock to his idea of proper submission to papal authority. In his *Supputationes* Erasmus wittily averred that if the pope were to approve the assertions of the arch-conservative and extravagant Noel Beda, he would appeal from the pope 'nodding' to the pope 'awake,' since 'black would not be white if the Roman Pontiff were to say so, which I know he will never do.' . . . (Ignatius' rule) is a rhetorical riposte to the terminology of Erasmus. " Ibid., p. 30.

12:3), and thus to believe in the Paschal Good News and in the Church that Jesus established incarnationally to continue his mission to bring the Kingdom to be, until he comes again. This same Holy Spirit, who acts within each person to lead them to God (cf. [23]) and who revealed to humanity the way to God ("gave the Ten Commandments"), guides the Church in its definitive proclamations. This is the faith that brings a person to love the Church deeply and to have an ecclesial mentality.[66] It is evident, once again, that Ignatius recognizes that the ecclesial mentality flows from the affective attitude of love for the Cnurch, as he repeats his imagery of Cnrist, the Spouse, and the Church, his spouse and our Holy Mother.

Second Consideration

The concrete issues that Ignatius refers to in these rules as instances of challenge to an ecclesial mentality in his own day refer particularly to Lutheran attacks and to positions argued by Erasmus.[67] In the same spirit, a director at present might point to contemporary issues that are a challenge to an ecclesial mentality today.[68] These are so many and so complex that it may perhaps be better to identify issues that arise from the experience of a particular retreatant.

---

66. The concreteness of the faith of Ignatius in the human community of the Church is shown by the very "scope of the Jesuit vocation" and is reflected in his understanding of ecclesial obedience. Cf. *Ibid.*, *pp.* 13-16; 18; 23-34; 81-82; 162-165. St. Augustine, who saw the Church as a community whose communion is union of hearts and minds flowing from the love of God, stressed that no authentic discernment can lead to a lack of unity with the Church, and that there can be no authentic love without love of unity, without love of the Church. Ibid., pp. 87-102.

67. Cf. the study by George E. Ganss, S.J., et al *Studies*, pp. 15-16.

68. See the "Rules for the Twentieth Century" by Ladislas Orsy, S.J., *Studies,* pp. 28-40, Cf. David L. Fleming, S.J., *The Spiritual Exercises of St. Ignatius: A Literal Translation and A Contemporary Reading* (St. Louis: The Institute of Jesuit Sources, 1978), pp. 231-237.

It is certainly correct, when needed by a retreatant, for the director to point out the Church's teaching that today the promotion of social justice is a constitutive element of the Gospel and intrinsic to authentic evangelization.

A rule of Ignatius possibly relevant to some retreatants at this time is his pointing out that both positive doctors and scholastic doctors should be praised [363]. Ignatius, reacting against Erasmus' attack on scholastic theologians, points out that these scholars have the ability to articulate revealed truths "according to the needs of our times." They have the advantage of advances in the study of Scripture and of the history of theology, as well as of the development of Church doctrine. By the same principle, the contributions of contemporary theologians now have the advantage of four centuries of progress since the time of Ignatius and, notably, of modern biblical theology and of the documents of Vatican II.

In helping a retreatant to deepen one's affective attitude of love for the Church and the consequent ecclesial mentality, the director, as always, will respond to the needs of each individual person and the insights and movements given to one by the Holy Spirit.

During the time of St. Thomas it was commonly taught at Paris that the knowledge necessary for the invisible mission of the Trinity within the human spirit must be more than mere informed faith. It must include a supernatural, spiritual *taste*. The Schoolmen often called this an affective or experimental knowledge—a "felt-knowledge" because it is linked to the affective experience of love and of spiritual delight. St. Thomas insisted that the just person's knowledge of the Divine Persons inhabiting one's spirit must be not solely informed faith but knowledge accompanied by love, that is to say, a felt-knowledge. He teaches that such knowledge belongs to wisdom: union with God through love, which provides the just person the basis for a just estimation of God and God's Creatures—the source of discernment. It is from this spiritual feeling that one learns to esteem correctly God and God's creatures. One learns divine things by experiencing them. Cf. John F. Dedek, *Experimental Knowledge of the Indwelling Trinity: An Historical Study of the Doctrine of St. Thomas* (Mundelein, Ill., 1958), especially pp. 146-148.

The tradition, as it has been handed down in Orthodoxy, is summarized by the great nineteenth century spiritual master, Theophane the Recluse. He insists that for real encounter with God, it is necessary that "the heart feels what the mind is thinking." *The Art of Prayer: An Orthodox Anthology,* Igumen Chariton of Valamo, trans. E. Kadloubovsky and E.M. Palmer (London and Boston: Faber and Faber, 1966), p. 67.

Chapter 9

Handbook's Conclusion

A THIRTY-DAY RETREAT PROVIDES AN OPPORTUNITY FOR A protracted period of being with God. This is true of both the retreatant and the director, in differing ways to be sure, as the director facilitates the meeting of the retreatant with God. When one is brought face-to-face with God for an entire month, something is bound to happen. The retreatant who generously enters into this dynamic cannot help deepening in knowledge of God and knowledge of self. It is almost impossible to be confronted with this knowledge and not experience a humble commitment growing out of it, a commitment that involves one in living henceforward out of the value system of Christ, a commitment that becomes highly apostolic. One does not get involved with Jesus Christ without being turned toward his people, in action as well as in thought and in prayer. One's vision of Christ present in the world today is heightened and clarified, and the desire, actually the need, to respond to that presence is intensified along with it. Herein lies the genius of the Exercises, and the apostolic spirit contained within.

The very life of Jesus Christ, contemplated in the quiet of the retreat, flows through the retreatant in newly experienced and less inhibited ways, not only developing the person's faith vision but enabling the person to draw upon the compassion of Christ, His wisdom, His energy, to continue His work of redemption. Thus energized by Christ through the experience of having his Spirit within, the person who has completed the exercises finds self changed, challenged, ready and confident on the deepest level of being, although facing the larger reality of the day-to-day world with some trepidation on other levels. Although the individual knows that there will be failures and often the lack of being one's best self, this awareness is not debilitating; it keeps the person grounded in humility. There is also the conviction that, experiencing the love of Christ which is beyond all knowledge of one's own weakness, the call to growth in and propagation of Christ's value system will still be there.

The retreatant has spent thirty days as a disciple, sitting at the feet of Jesus Christ and learning from him. Now the disciple becomes the apostle, going forth in Christ's name and filled with his Spirit. Entering into the Exercises is an adventure and moving out of the retreat is a continuance of the same adventure. Although one might have felt very much of an apostle before the retreat, at its conclusion the person has come to a new realization of what this means for him or her now, in whatever concrete situation. Bonded by the common experience, the director and the retreatant often continue to be in mutual support for each other after the retreat.

Just as it proved a difficult task, in some ways, to write this handbook, so it is difficult to bring it to conclusion. There is so much more one could say about the Exercises. Even during the time it took to commit to paper the material in these pages, there has continued to be growth in an understanding of Ignatius and the Spiritual Exercises. So it is hard to conclude with any finality of "That's it."

But one cannot write forever. It is now our hope that a director having become acquainted with this *Handbook* will find it a ready source of information, inspiration, and general assistance in the privilege of guiding a retreatant through the *Spiritual Exercises* of St. Ignatius of Loyola.

PART IV

Reference Materials

Suggested Readings

Alphonso, Herbert, S.J., *The Personal Vocation: Transformation in Depth Through the Spiritual Exercises*, Rome, Italy: Centrum Ignatianum Spiritualis, 1990.

Coathalem, Herve. *Ignatian Insights.* A Guide to the Complete Spiritual Exercises. Taichung (Taiwan): Kuangchi Press, 1971.

English, S.J., John. *Choosing Life,* New York: Paulist Press, 1978.

_____. *Spiritual Freedom*, Guelph, Ontario, Loyola House, 1973.

Fleming, S.J., David L. *The Spiritual Exercises of St. Ignatius: A Literal Translation and a Contemporary Reading.* St. Louis: The Institute of Jesuit Sources, 1978.

_____ (Ed.). *Notes on the Spiritual Exercises of St. Ignatius of Loyola: The Best of the Review.* St. Louis: Review for Religious, 1981.

Ganss, George E., S.J., *The Spiritual Exercises of St. Ignatius: A Translation and Commentary,* St. Louis: The Institute of Jesuit Sources, 1992.

La Frank, Alex. "Freedom for Service; How to Use the Individually Guided Spiritual Exercises." Supplement to *Progressio* 3 (April, 1974), Rome.

Laplace, S.J., Jean. *An Experience of Life in the Spirit,* Chicago: Franciscan Herald Press, 1977.

_____. *Preparing for Spiritual Direction,* Chicago: Franciscan Herald Press, 1975.

Magaña, S.J., José. *Ignatian Exercises: A Strategy for Liberation.* Hicksville, N.Y.: Exposition Press, 1974.

Schmitt, S.J., Robert L. "The Christ Experience and Relationship Fostered in the Spiritual Exercises of St. Ignatius of Loyola." *Studies in the Spirituality of Jesuits* VI, No. 5, (October, 1974).

Soundings. A Task Force on Social Consciousness and Ignatian Spirituality. Washington, D.C.: Center for Concern, 1974.

Tetlow, Joseph A., S.J., *Choosing Christ in the World: Directing the Spiritual Exercises of St. Ignatius Loyola According to Annotations Eighteen and Nineteen,* St. Louis: The Institute of Jesuit Sources, 1989.

_____. *Ignatius Loyola: Spiritual Exercises,* New York: Crossroad, 1992.

Ongoing helps in directing the Spiritual Exercises are published regularly in:

Studies in the Spirituality of Jesuits, St. Louis, Missouri.

Supplements to *The Way.* London.

Review for Religious. St. Louis, Missouri.

Appendix One

Preparation for the Thirty-day Spiritual Exercises

It is truly impossible to make the thirty-day Spiritual Exercises unless one is well prepared to enter into them with the necessary dispositions.[1] Ignatius himself was very careful about this. When it was possible to give adequate preparation before the beginning of the retreat, he would simply give the Principle and Foundation [23] on the first day, in order to enable the retreatant to bring to vivid consciousness the vision and grace already given. The same evening, he would begin the First Week. On the other hand, if the retreatant did not yet have the grace of the Principle and Foundation, Ignatius would devote more time to it.[2]

The director must not give the First Week until he or she is certain that the retreatant is properly disposed, even if this preparation period takes most of the thirty days. Should this be the case, the director should encourage the retreatant, if possible, to continue making the Exercises according to number 19 of the Introductory Observations, sometimes called the "Nineteenth Annotation Retreat" or the "Retreat during Daily Life."[3]

---

1. See "Dynamics of Directing and Making the Spiritual Exercises of St. Ignatius of Loyola," in Part I.

2. For an excellent, documented summary of the practice of Ignatius and its rationale, see Gilles Cusson, S.J., *Pedagogie de l'experience spirituelle personelle*, (Paris: DDB, 1968), pp. 65-71.

Some directors will not accept a retreatant for the thirty-day Spiritual Exercises unless it is possible to give six months of preparation through appropriate Scriptural prayer and through regular spiritual direction. At the present time, however, many directors find that the first meeting with a retreatant can take place only on the eve of its beginning. When this is the case, the initial conversation of the director with the retreatant is of vital importance in order to know where to begin.

Directors develop their own way of proceeding in this initial conversation. My own approach, after preliminary "getting to know you" talk, is to pose the following questions:

1. Background

How old are you?

If a religious—how long have you been so? Tell me about the spirit of your congregation.

If a lay person—are you single or married? Any children? What is your sense of Christian vocation in your life situation?

How is your general physical and emotional health? Any special needs with respect to diet, rest, and so on?

Right now, do you feel healthy and rested, and ready to begin the retreat?

How do you feel about God? About others? About yourself? (During this part of the conversation, I try to come to some preliminary assessment of the level of maturity of the person, and whether one has any attitudinal or theoretical "hangups" that could be obstacles to the dynamic movement of the Spiritual Exercises.)

What kind of retreats have you made before? Any directed retreats? In general, have your past retreats been positive or negative experiences?

---

3. See Appendix 4.

When was your last retreat? What were its chief graces? Do you feel that you have lived out of these?

2. Prayer history

How do you pray now? Any special focus in your prayer? Special images? Key words or phrases?

Tell me about your images of God. Of Jesus.

Are you familiar with Scriptural prayer? What are your favorite Scripture passages?

3. Dispositions for this retreat

What, right now, do you want to get out of this retreat?

Where do you feel yourself to be right now before the Lord?

Any fears entering retreat?

Any "brokenness" that you are aware of?

Areas where you cling to the familiar—where "practical atheism" begins, and hope is lacking?[4]

Should there be a possibility of some days or weeks of preparation before actually beginning the retreat, I enter into the above conversation at our first meeting, which starts that preparation. I also ask the person to prepare by doing what I call the "exercise in dynamic memory" during the days or weeks before the retreat.

This exercise is intended to aid a person to bring to awareness his or her ongoing faith experience of God, to put an individual in touch with one's own "sacred history" and the pattern of the workings of God in one's own life. Dynamic memory is

---

4. Persons can unwittingly fall into "practical atheism" when, although they do not deny the existence of God theoretically, they live as if God did not exist, for example, clinging to creatures for basic security, or losing Christian hope when a situation seems humanly hopeless.

not mere calendar memory, as if one reached back in time in a linear fashion to isolated biographical events. It is, rather, looking into one's ongoing *life:* the past events that I carry with me now as part of my present, ever-expanding selfawareness. The person is invited, therefore, using dynamic memory, to seek to identify those moments throughout life when, at least now on reflection, one can say, "I know that God was present to me in that moment." Thus, the person looks for those moments of great light or of great joy, of the felt presence of God in the events of life through people or places or circumstances. One also remembers the "paschal events" of one's own life: events which, at the time, were experienced as clinging to the rock and bleeding or as climbing Calvary, but which God has already turned into sources of true life and of knowing the divine presence. One does not at this time look at memories that still need to be healed, that have not yet been touched paschally by the Lord. This exercise is an extended *Magnificat:* reflecting upon the wonderful things that God has done in me, a humble servant. What still needs to be redeemed will surface during the retreat.

Having brought to conscious awareness these great moments, simply as they entered into memory, the person can now, if enough days are available, arrange them in chronological order, filling in further details that will arise during this remembering. One now has a sketch of one's spiritual autobiography, one's own sacred history. Now, the person should try to see how these experiences of the presence of God have shaped the pattern of his or her own sacred history—the beginning, the middle, and the end of the action of God in life that enables one to discern when the Lord is truly calling to an election, and to detect the deceptive movements of selfish love and of evil within self [333].[5]

---

5. A more extensive development of "dynamic memory" will be found in my "Ignatian Discernment," *Studies in the Spirituality of Jesuits,* vol. II, no. 2, (April, 1970), pp. 77-82.

Until the beginning of the retreat, I also suggest that the person pray over Scripture texts on the reality, majesty, love, and unending fidelity of God, and on texts showing how God calls an individual. All this leads the person toward praying for the grace of the Principle and Foundation [23].[6]

Finally, I urge the person to relax, waste time, and get much rest and sleep before the beginning of the retreat.

When the time comes to actually begin the retreat, during the first meeting with the retreatant, I invite him or her to share with me the results of the dynamic memory exercise. This greatly helps my ability to direct this person, since it provides much background which, otherwise, would take a long time to surface. I ask the person to share with me the movements and insights experienced during the Scriptural prayer. Finally, I repeat the question—quite often the answer now is different than in our first conversation—What, right now, do you want to get out of this retreat?

I either select particular texts to suggest to the person for prayer or I simply give a copy of the following list to the person for his or her own choosing of texts for prayer during the days or weeks of preparation.

1. *An Interior Exodus to Seek God*—Wisd. 8:17-9:18; Pss. 40, 95, 100, 139; Isa. 48:12-19; 51:48; Matt. 7:7-11; Luke 8:4-15; Eph. 1:17-19.

2. *The Call of the Lord*—Gen. 12:1-3, 17:1-22; Exod. chaps. 3, 18,33; Deut. 30:15-20; 1 Sam. 3:1-14; Isa. chap. 6; Jer. chap. 1, 20:7-18; Ezek. chaps. 1-3, chaps. 8-10; Dan. 7-12; Matt. chap. 13, 20:1-16, 21:33-43, 22:10-14; Luke 1:26-38; Acts 9:1-19; Rom. 8:29-39, 9:24-33; 1 Cor. 1:26-31; Gal. 1:11-19; Eph. 1:4-14; 2 Thess. 2:13-14; 2 Tim. 1:9-14; James 2:5; 1 Pet. 2:3-10, 5:10-11; Rev. 3:19-22.

---

6. See "Dynamics of the First Principle and Foundation," in Part II.

3. *God the Creator*—Gen. chap. 102; Job chaps.36-41; Wisd. 9:1-4, 13:1-9; Eccles. (Sir.) 39:12-22, 42:15-25, 43:1-33; Pss. 19, 48, 92, 95, 104; Rom. 1:1923; 1 Cor. 1:20-31.

4. *God's Power, Majesty and Holiness*—Eccles. (Sir.) 33:7-15; Lev. 11:44-45, 19:1-2; 2 Sam. 22:8-16; 1 Chron. 29:11-18; Job chaps. 38-42; Isa. 29:15-17, 40:12-31, 45:9-13; Jer. 18:1-12; Pss. 99,104; Matt. 5:43-48; Luke 1:49; James 1:13; Rev. 4:8.

5. *God's Fatherliness*—Hos. 11:1-11; Isa. 63:16; Jer. 3:19, 31:9; Wisd. 2:13-18; Matt. 5:43-48, 6:1-18, 26-34; 10:29-31; Luke 11:1-13; John 1:12-13, 20:17.

6. *God's Goodness*—Num. 23:19; Isa. chap. 12, 54:10; Jer. 31:1-6; Pss. 106, 116, 136, 137, 144.

7. *The Human Person in the Image of God*—Deut. 30:11-14; Wisd. 2:23; Eccles. (Sir.) 17:1-13; Isa. 43:1-7; Ps. 8; Rom. 8:29-30; 2 Cor. 3:18; Col. 3:10; 1 John 3:1-3.

Appendix Two

Ignatius on Spiritual Direction

IN THE INTRODUCTORY OBSERVATIONS [1-20] AND THE FOL-
lowing Presupposition [22], Ignatius has also provided an excellent manual for ongoing spiritual direction. Globally, this can be
seen as follows:

I. A focus is identifiable within the Introductory Observations:

1. The dynamic movement of Christian spiritual life is indicated as PURIFICATION enabling TOTAL SURRENDER
   TO GOD [1].

2. There is a need to adapt direction to each individual person
   [4]; [6]; [8]; [9]; [11]; [13]; [14]; [18]; [19].

3. Direction is above all *listening* and leaving room for the
   action of the Holy Spirit [7]; [15]; see also [22], the Presupposition.

4. There is a way to present matter to a directee [2].

5. The director must help the person to clarify one's experience and to discern [6]; [16]; [17].

6. The director assists the person to focus one's whole body-
   person on the Lord in prayer [3]; [5]; [6]; [12]; [13]; [14];
   [18]; [19]; see also [73-90], the Additional Directions.

II. The twofold dynamic movement of Christian spiritual life is outlined in [1] of the Introductory Observations:

1. *PURIFICATION* ". . . preparing and disposing the soul to rid itself of all inordinate attachments"; thus, spiritual direction should help the person grow into spiritual freedom;

2. *CONCRETE SURRENDER TO THE MYSTERY OF GOD AT ALL TIMES* "after their removal . . . seeing and finding the will of God in the disposition of our life for the salvation of our soul"; thus, spiritual direction should help the person to discern the will of God for ordering one's whole life to holiness—union with God.

III. Ignatius states the prerequisites for entering into the dynamic movement of Christian spiritual life:

1. In number 5 of the Introductory Observations, one must have, at least as an ideal, the desire to surrender to God, which presupposes personal realization of the reality and majesty as well as love of God.

2. In number 12 of the Introductory Observations, one must make a practical commitment to cooperate with the grace of God, above all, fidelity to prayer even when it is difficult.

3. This latter is reinforced in number 6 by its insistence upon diligent observance of the Additional Directions [73-90], which consciously use the effect of environment and of the body upon states of consciousness and vice-versa. The body, imagination, and feelings must be focused upon the mystery contemplated, and bodily and psychological environment must be brought to bear in the same way.

IV. For spiritual direction to be effective, it is necessary that both directee and director are not judgmental of one another.

Should it be necessary to correct or to clear up misapprehensions or ignorance, this must be done with love [22].

V. The successive Introductory Observations are a collection of wise maxims for any spiritual direction. (The statements in uppercase letters are indications for ongoing spiritual direction. I have derived these from the content of the Ignatian text, summarized in lowercase.)

[2] DO NOT SPEAK MUCH. ALLOW THE HOLY SPIRIT TO WORK. Give the method and order of meditations and contemplations. Narrate briefly, giving short explanations. Greater spiritual relish and fruit result for the person in treating with God oneself.

[3] HELP THE PERSON'S MOTIVATION TO SINCERE EFFORT TO GROW SPIRITUALLY. Greater reverence is required when praying: the whole self focused on God. Check on this.

[4] DO NOT HAVE *A PRIORI* EXPECTATIONS OF THE PACE OF SPIRITUAL GROWTH. FOLLOW THE MOVEMENT OF THE HOLY SPIRIT IN EACH PERSON. Adapt the length of time of each stage of the Exercises to each person. Achieve the goal of each stage before moving on to the next.

[5] HELP THE PERSON TO GROW IN THE NECESSARY BASIC ATTITUDES FOR SPIRITUAL GROWTH. There is need for sincere, generous effort.

[6] ASK QUESTIONS TO HELP THE PERSON TO CLARIFY HIS OR HER OWN SPIRITUAL EXPERIENCES. If no movements are experienced, investigate the fidelity to the exercises and the Additional Directions.

[7] BE GENTLE AND KIND DURING TIMES OF TRIAL, NOT JUDGMENTAL, BUT ENCOURAGING. When the

retreatant is in desolation, be gentle, kind, encouraging, thus helping the person to dispose oneself for consolation.

[8] INTRODUCE INFORMATION ABOUT SPIRITUAL GROWTH AS IT IS REQUIRED. Explain the Rules for Discernment of Spirits I [313-327] and II [328-336] as the experience of the retreatant requires them.

[9] ADAPT INFORMATION AND CHALLENGES TO THE PERSON'S READINESS. It is harmful to introduce the Rules for Discernment of Spirits II before the retreatant has achieved the fruit of the First Week.

[10] KEEP PACE IN DIRECTION WITH THE PACE OF GROWTH OF THE PERSON. Help the retreatant to detect evil under the appearance of good with the Rules for Discernment of Spirits II.

[11] HELP THE PERSON NOT TO DREAM OF THE FUTURE, BUT TO MEET GOD HERE AND NOW. Focus where the retreatant is—for example, the First Week—without leaping ahead to the Second Week.

[12] BE EXIGENT ABOUT FIDELITY TO PRAYER. One should pray for five hours a day and stick to it. The heart of the matter is to give God time to work spiritual growth.

[13] INSIST ON FIDELITY TO PRAYER ESPECIALLY IN TIMES OF DRYNESS. Pray longer when in desolation.

[14] HELP THE PERSON TO DISCERN AUTHENTICALLY AND NOT RASHLY, ESPECIALLY WHEN ONE IS FEELING FERVENT. Watch individual temperament. See to it that response and decision do not come from unconsidered fervor, but from real discernment.

[15] DO NOT PERSUADE THE PERSON TO A DECISION. BE AN OBJECTIVE MIRROR. The director should take a neutral stance toward the retreatant's decision, leaving room for the Holy Spirit to work with the individual. The director

must remain in equilibrium, like a scale, allowing the Spirit to work directly with the person and the person directly with the Spirit.

[16] HELP THE PERSON TO GROW TOWARD TRUE FREE-DOM BY ASKING QUESTIONS, POSING CHALLENGES, ETC. Help the retreatant to recognize selfish desires and to pray for the opposite—not to wish for anything, unless the Spirit orders one's desires, so that the only cause to desire anything will be to respond to God.

[17] REQUIRE REAL OPENNESS TO THE DIRECTOR AS A CONDITION FOR GIVING DIRECTION. Help the retreatant to recognize the need for total openness to the director, so that the director can be of help by knowing where the person is and how the Spirit is working with him or her, and adapt exercises and direction accordingly.

[18] ALWAYS ADAPT ALL FACETS OF SPIRITUAL DIREC-TION TO *THIS* UNIQUE, INDIVIDUAL PERSON. What is given during the Exercises depends upon who the retreatant is, also where and how, and what he or she wants.

[19] MAKE EVEN EXTRAORDINARY ADAPTATIONS IN DIRECTION FOR PERSONS IN EXTRAORDINARY CIRCUMSTANCES. It is possible to give the Spiritual Exercises over a long period of time, while the retreatant continues his or her regular occupation in daily life.

[20] ACCORDING TO POSSIBILITIES, ENCOURAGE THE DIRECTEE AT TIMES TO HAVE A REAL "DESERT" EXPERIENCE. The Spiritual Exercises are best made full time, when all of one's energy can be focused on dialogue with God in solitude and silence.

It should be especially noted that number 17 of the Introductory Observations is really the key to direction. It establishes the "ground of dialogue" within which all else is operative. Notice that the retreatant or directee is to keep the director informed of all the spiritual movements that one experiences. The aim is authentic discernment. The various techniques and exercises of the retreat and of the spiritual direction have value only inasmuch as they help improve the quality of the spiritual experience they foster by helping the person to dispose self for the saving encounter with the Father through Jesus Christ in the Holy Spirit and for authentic discernment of the response to which one is called in this encounter.[7]

---

7. For an excellent treatment of spiritual direction that can be very helpful for the directee as well as the director, see Jean Laplace, S.J., *Preparing for Spiritual Direction* (Chicago: Franciscan Herald Press, 1975).

Appendix Three

Scripture Texts for Spiritual Reading During the Spiritual Exercises

IGNATIUS SUGGESTS THAT DURING THE CONTEMPLATIONS OF the mysteries of the life of Jesus, it can be helpful to read passages from the *Imitation of Christ* or the Gospels, and from the lives of the saints [100]. At times the director will know of some particular reading matter that would be very good for an individual retreatant at a given point within the movement of the Spiritual Exercises. Otherwise, my own bias is to suggest that one read only Scripture texts, doing that slowly and reflectively, allowing the written Word of God to deepen the insights and movements being received from the Holy Spirit.

Consequently, I give the retreatant lists of helpful Scripture texts according to the stage of the Exercises where one now is. The following list can provide a director with such suggested spiritual reading, as well as with indications of texts for the actual prayer periods within the movement of the Exercises, and also for prayer following the retreat. It is essential that a director pray over texts oneself, in order to know by experience which can be appropriate for *this* retreatant at this time. The more retreatants a director has directed, the greater his or her familiarity with fitting Scripture texts will become. Ultimately what forms a good director is experience.

THE FIRST WEEK [24-90]

First Exercise [45-54]

Atmosphere—	Bar. 1:15-3:8 (Prayer of the Exiles). Sin—John 3:19-21; Matt. chap. 23.
Sin of the Angels [50]—	Satan: pride leading to "no"—Jude vv. 6-7; Luke 4:1-13; John 8:44; Rev. chap. 12.
Sin of Adam and Eve [51]—	the human heart given over to other gods—Gen. chap. 3.
Sin of Any Person [52]—	Pss. 54, 58; Rom. chaps. 1- 1 1 .

Second Exercise [55-61]

Contrition—	Pss. 25, 38, 39, 51; Eccles.(Sir.) 17:4-18:21; Acts 2:37-39; 1 John 1:5-10.
Change of Heart—	Isa. 58:1-12; Jer. 7:1-8, 31:31-34; Ezek. 11:17-20; 18:30-31; Matt. 3:1-12; Luke 24:46-47; John 12:24-25; Acts 2:37-39; Eph. 4:20-24.
Mercy and Forgiveness—	Pss. 62, 63, 141, 143; Isa. 49:13, 63:7-64:12; Hos. 11:1-11; Wisd. 11:2312:2; Matt. 8:1-17; Mark 1:40-45; Luke 7:36-50, 19:1-10; Rom. chap. 5; Phil. 2:5-11; 1 John 2:1.
Scriptural Metaphor—	Ezek. chap. 16.
Healing Texts—	(a) Possessed—Matt. 4:24, 10:1, 12:22-29; Mark 1:32-34, 5:1-20, 9:14-29; Luke 4:31-37;
	(b) Sick—Matt. 8:1-17, 9:1-8, 18-37, 12:9-21, 15:21-31, 20:29-34; Mark 10:46-52; Luke 7:1-10, 13:10-17, 17:11-19; John 4:43-54, 5:1-15, chap. 9.
	(c) Dead—Matt. 9:18-25; Luke 7:11-17; John chap. 11.

Bridge Day from First to Second Week

Grace to pray for: A profound desire for Jesus Christ to come to you in a very real and personal way as *your* Savior and Healer, and as Savior and Healer of the sinful world.

> Isa. 7:10-17, 9:2-7, 10:33-11:10, 12:1-6, 25:9, 26:9, 29:18-21, 32:1--4, 35:1-10, 40:1-11, 42:10-19, 52:7-12.
> Mic. 4:1-8, 7:7-20.

THE KINGDOM OF CHRIST [91-99]

Overview—	Eph. chaps. 1-3.
The Servant—	Isa. chaps. 40-55, especially the Servant Songs: 42:1-9, 49:1-6, 60:4-11, 52:13-53:12.
The Messiah—	Pss. 72, 110; Luke 3:1-9, 4:14-32; John 1:19-34; Col. 1:13-20.
The King—	Pss. 2, 45; Isa. 9:2-7, chaps. 11, 12; Jer. 23:1-8; Ezek. chap. 34; Zech. 9:9-10; Rev. 19: 11-16.
The True Priest—	Heb. chaps. 5, 8-10:9.
The Call of the King [95]—	Matt. 20:20-28, 28: 16-20; Mark 10:35-45; Luke 5:1-11; John 14:1, 15:20, 16:20, 33; Acts 1:4-11; Rom. chap. 5,6; 1 Cor. 15: 20-28; Phil. chap. 2; Col 3:4; Rev. 11:15.
The Oblation [98]—	Phil. 3:7-11.

THE SECOND WEEK [101-189]

(Note: Read only as far as the mystery being contemplated.)

First Contemplation: Incarnation [101-109]

Background—	Exod. chaps. 3, 4; Dan. chap. 9; Zeph. 3:14-17.
First Point [106]—	John 1:1-14.

Second Point [107]— Rom. 3:11-18.
Third Point [108]— Ezek. 32:18-32.

Second Contemplation: Life at Nazareth [134], [271]

Humble, Human Virtues—	Books of Wisdom, Proverbs, Ecclesiasticus (Sirach).
Ideal of Human Wisdom—	Eccles. (Sir.) chaps. 1-15.
Counsels of St. Paul—	Rom. 12:3-13; 1 Thess. 4:1012, 5:14; Philemon.
Psalms at Nazareth—	"The Law in Jesus"—Ps. 119; Providence: The Father watching Jesus—Ps. 33.
When God Erupts into a Life—	Gen 12; 1 Sam. 2: 12-3:21; Isa. chap. 6; Jer. 1:4-16. Psalm 27.

Meditation of Two Standards [136-148]

Servant Songs of Isaiah—	42:1-9, 49:1-6; 50:4-11, 52:13-53:12.
Rev. chaps. 13-14.	
The Two Days: Discernment—	Deut. 30:15-20; Ps. 42; Luke 12:54-59; John 1:10-11, chap. 7; Rom 12:1-2, 1 Cor. chaps. 13-14; 2 Cor. 11:12-15; Eph. 6:10-20; Col. 3:1-4; Phil. 1:9-11; I Thess. 5:19-22; Heb. 5:11-14.
Christian Wisdom—	1 Cor. chaps. 1-4.
Christ's Program—	Matt. chaps. 5-7.
Colloquy [147]—	Gen. 22:1-19, 32:24-33; Luke 1:26-38.

Temptations of Christ [161], [274]

	Exod. 13:17-15:21; Isa. chaps. 63-64; 1 Cor. 1:17-2:15; Phil. 2:6-10.

Three Classes of Persons [149-157]

Some Summary Texts—	John 1:5, 8:44; Acts 26:18; 1 Cor. chap. 15; 2 Cor. 2:11, 4:4, 6:16, 11-14; Eph. 5:6-14; 6:10-20: Col. 1:13-14: 1 Tim. 6:3-16.
How Do I Respond?—	Eccles. (Sir.) 2:1-18: Matt. 13:44-46; Luke 9:57-62, 14:25-35, 18:18-34, James 1:2-25.

The Ministry of Christ [275-288]

Formation of the Apostles—	a progressive growth process of discovery of the mystery of the Cross: (a) Peter—(1) John 1:40-42; (2) Luke 5:1-11; (3) Matt. 14:22-23; (4) John 6:59-70; (5) Matt. 16:13-28; (6) Matt. 18:21-22; (7) John 21:15-23. (b) the Apostles—(1) Luke 9:22-26; (2) Mark 8:31-38; (3) Matt. 16:21-27; (4) Luke 9:43-49; (5) Mark 9:30-50; (6) Matt. 17:22-23; (7) John 12:23-26. Cf. 1 and 2 Tim.
Ideal of the Apostolic Life—	Luke chaps. 9-10; Acts 3:1-16.

Pattern of Jesus Christ: Exemplar for All Christians

Service of Others—	Mark 10:43-45.
In Fraternal Love—	John 13:34, 15:12-15; Eph. 5:1-2.
Who Makes Unity—	John 17:11, 20-23, chap. 21.
Humility—	John 13:12-17; Rom. 15:1-3.
Patience in Suffering—	1 Pet. 2:20-23.

Last Day of the Second Week

Lazarus—	John 12:1-10.
Psalms—	Zech. 9:9-17; Mark 11:1-10; Luke 19:2944; John 12:12-19.

Nothing Can Stop God—	Num. 22:23-25.
The Hour—	John 12:20-50.
End of the Temple and End of Time—	Matt. chaps. 24-25; Mark 13:1-37; Luke 21:5-36.
Psalms of "Going Up"—	120-134.

THE THIRD WEEK [190-217]

First Contemplation: Eucharist [190-199]; [289]

Institution Narratives—	Matt. 26:26-29; Mark 14:22-25; Luke 22:17-19.
Related Texts—	Pss. 23, 111, 118, 136, 145; Rom. chap. 12; 1 Cor. 1:17-2:16,

Second Contemplation: Agony in the Garden [200-203]; [290]

	Ps. 69; Matt. 20:17-23.
Arrest of Jesus [208]; [291]—	Pss. 60, 61; Jer. 11:18-19, 12:4, 18:18-20, 20:7-18, 23:9-40, chap. 26, 38:13.
Denial by Peter [208]; [291]—	Reread formation of Peter texts above.
Jesus before the Powerful (Caiaphas, Sanhedrin, Pilate, Herod soldiers) [208]; [291-297]—	Pss. 2, 26; Isa. 63:1-6, chaps. 49-55; Jer. 18:18; 1 Tim. 6:13.
Way of the Cross [208]; [296-297]—	Pss. 22, 59,, 71, 88; Jer. 11:18-19, 20:7-18; John 13:12-20, 12:2336; Liturgy of Good Friday, especially the Adoration of the Cross.
The Crowd [291-297]—	Wisd. 2:10-3:9; 1 Cor. 2:7; Rev. 11:1-13.

Before the Cross [208]; [296-297].	*The Father*—SILENCE . . . Pss. 55, 57, 75. Ourselves—Isa. 52:13-15, chap. 53; Lamentations of Jeremiah; Eccles. (Sir.) 36:1-17; Heb. 9:14.
The Death [208]; [297]—	Pss. 22, 31 40, 56, 59, 61, 69, 70, 88, 109, 141; in sequence 69-75; Zech. 11:13; Rom. 5:10, 6:10, 8:3, chaps. 1-11; Phil. 2: 1-9; Heb. 2:7-18; 1 John 5:5-12.
Before Christ in the Tomb [208]; [298]—	Pss. 4,27, 28, 77.

THE FOURTH WEEK [218-229]; [299-312]

Christ—	Pss. 3, 16, 30, 76, 113-116; Rom. 1:1-7; Easter Liturgy.
Mary—	Isa. 54:4-10; Song of Songs.
Resurrection—	Pss. 24, 29, 46, 47, 48, 68, 87, 97, 101, 146; John chaps. 13-17; Acts 2:22-36; 1 Cor. chaps. 12-15; all of Ephesians; 2 Pet. chap. 1; 1 John; Rev. chaps. 19-22.
Ascension [312]—	Pss. 24, 29, 47, 97.
Contemplation to Attain Love of God [230-237]—	Jer. 31:35-37; John chap. 14, 15:1-7; 1 Cor. 8:2-3; chap. 13; 2 Cor. 2:18; Pss. 93, 135, 136, 138, 147, 149, 150; 1 John 3:1-4.
Christ Will Come Again—	Pss. 120-134, 137; Isa. chaps. 54-55, 65:13-25, chap. 66; Rev. chaps 21-22.

* * * *

Addenda to Readings for the Second Week and the Third Week

A Synthesis of the Gospel According to St. Matthew

I. BEGINNING—

"Do penance, the Kingdom is near"—4:17

Christ's Qualifications: Sovereign power—11:26-27; Authority over the Sabbath—12:1-7; Transfiguration—17:1-8; Lord of David—22:41-46; Gentle, humble comforter—11:28-30; 14:15-21; 15:32-39.

II. REQUIREMENT OF ABSOLUTE FAITH, BLIND TRUST

Centurion—8:13; sea: "little faith"—8:23-37; woman with hemorrhage—9:18-22; blind man—9:27-31; Capernaum—13:58; Peter on water—14:22-33; Canaanite woman—15:21-28; demonic boy—17:14-21; move mountains—21:18-22.

III. REQUIREMENT OF ABSOLUTE DETACHMENT TO FOLLOW HIM

Leave the dead—8:18-22; Matthew left his business and followed—9:9; Caesar's, God's—22:15-22.

IV. HIS MISSION

To call sinners—9:10-13; 12:7; compassion, laborers for harvest—9:36-38; do the will of God—12:46-50; foretelling Passion and Resurrection—17:22-23; 20:17-19; his mission given to us—28: 16-20.

V. HOW TO DO HIS WORK

Preach the Kingdom; evangelical poverty; persecution; inspired by the Spirit, hold to the end; be treated like the Master; no fear; proclaim from housetops; trust; not peace, but the sword; if affections for others greater than for me, not worthy of me; take up cross; give up life—10:5-42; fraternal correction—18:15-17; common prayer—18:19-20; celibacy for those called—19:10-12; to be perfect, sell all, follow me—19:16-22; leave brothers, sisters, father, mother, children—19:29-30; Kingdom taken by violence—11:12.

VI. REQUIREMENT OF HUMILITY

Revealed to little ones—11:25; like little children—18:1-4; theirs is the Kingdom—19:13-15; make self least—20:20-28; greatest must be servant—23:1-12.

VII. NEED OF SINCERITY—15:1-9; 15:15-20; 23:13-39.

VIII. PARABLES

Chap. 13:1-23—*Sower* (hearing the message means to *live* it); chaps. 24-30; 36-40—*Weeds* (the world and judgment); chaps. 31-33—*Mustard Seed; leaven* (Kingdom grows from a small start: *hearing* message); chaps. 44-46—*Treasure, pearl* (absolute detachment for the Kingdom); chaps. 47-50—*Dragnet of fish* (judgment); chaps. 51-52—*New things and old* (Teacher of the Kingdom); 18:21-35—*Merciless debtor* (forgive as forgiven—"Our Father"); 20:1-16—*Vineyard; Kingdom* (last first; first last); 21:28-32—*Two sons and vineyard* (need of action); 21:33-46—*Vinedressers kill son* (rejection of Pharisees); 22:1-14—*Wedding* (rejection; need of grace); 25:1-15—*Wise and foolish virgins* (*always* be ready to meet Christ); 25:14-30— *Talents* (need to respond).

IX. THE CROSS—THE PLAN OF THE FATHER

"Get behind me, Satan" . . . "Follow me"—16:21-28; to be betrayed, killed, rise—17:22-23; 26:1-2; persecuted because you profess my name—24:4-10.

X. THE GREAT COMMANDMENT—22:34-40

Charity and judgment—25:31-46.

Appendix Four

The Nineteenth Annotation Retreat

IN THE *SPIRITUAL EXERCISES,* ST. IGNATIUS HIMSELF DESIGNED a wonderfully effective adaptation of the thirty-day Exercises for persons who cannot be free to devote thirty days to making them [19]. In this retreat "in daily life," the exercitant continues the ordinary schedule of work or study and normal social life, but commits self to a daily prayer period in order to move through the dynamic of the Spiritual Exercises over a period of weeks or months. Undoubtedly describing his own experience of directing this retreat, Ignatius suggests an hour and a half prayer period daily and specifies one day for each point of the First [45-54], Second [55-61], and Fifth Exercises [65-71], with the use of the ten Additional Directions [73-90]. Then the retreatant moves into the Second Week.[1]

In accord with the Ignatian basic principle of adaptation to each individual retreatant, it is found today, in practice, that the commitment of time for a daily prayer period may vary from half an hour or less to an hour and a half or more for a particular retreatant. The daily life schedule of some persons is such that they find it best to pray for half an hour in the morning and for another half hour in the evening. The director sees the

---

1. For an excellent detailed presentation of the retreat in daily life, see Gilles Cusson, *Conduit-moi sur le chemin d'eternite Les Exercises dans la vie courante* (2 edition, Montreal: Les Editions Bellarmin, 1976).

retreatant once a week, or more or less frequently, according to circumstances. The essential for this retreat is that the person gradually move through the entire dynamic or the spiritual Exercises, however long a time this may take according to the individual's pattern of daily life and to the movements of the holy Spirit within one.

Directors of the Nineteenth Annotation Retreat find that their direction follows the dynamic of direction during a thirty-day retreat. Spiritual movements are reported by the retreatant and, as the successive graces are received, one moves the retreatant through the First Principle and Foundation to the First Week and through the rest of the Exercises, just as the director does during a thirty-day retreat. In order to direct the Nineteenth Annotation Retreat effectively and confidently, it is very helpful to be an experienced director of thirty-day retreats.

The Nineteenth Annotation Retreat can be an excellent instrument for the spiritual formation of diocesan seminarians or for young religious particularly in preparation for ordination to the diaconate or for profession of vows. It can provide a splendid infrastructure for the development of a regular rhythm of prayer and of ongoing spiritual growth for diocesan priests or religious or lay persons unable to make a thirty-day retreat. An actual advantage of this retreat in daily life is the occasion it provides for the ongoing integration of all the events of one's life situation into a continual discerning of response to the Lord and a growing toward finding God in all things. It can provide marvelous follow-up to the experience of an eight day directed retreat.

The "game plan" of a Nineteenth Annotation Retreat is actually that of the Exercises as described in this handbook, adapted to the circumstances of a retreat in daily life. Thus, the following notes are simply a description of an experience of directing such a retreat as an example of one way of moving through this retreat with a person.

1. With this retreatant, it was possible to begin with an eight-day directed retreat. The entire eight days were spent in preparation for and prayer to receive the grace of the First Principle and Foundation [23]. Then the retreatant began the Nineteenth Annotation Retreat and spent the next two weeks deepening that grace through praying over appropriate Scripture passages with the aid of the following exercise.

"An Exercise on the Principle and Foundation of the Spiritual Exercises of St. Ignatius of Loyola"

Grace to be prayed for: inasmuch as my response to aspects within the text is not an absolute "Yes," I ask the grace to respond to each with an absolute "Yes."

Dwell upon each truth. It can be helpful to pray over Scripture texts that develop each truth. Then, in the presence of God and asking the light of the Holy Spirit, answer the questions. It can be helpful to write down these answers for subsequent reflection and for focusing your prayer for the grace to be able to answer an absolute "Yes."

    I. God IS!

    Do I experience this as *the* most overwhelming reality?

    II. God is LOVE!

    Have I truly *realized* this?

    III. God CREATES to *communicate Divine love* through human beings, loving all creatures with God's own love.

    Do I see all creatures—myself, other people, all things—in this light?

    IV. So, ALL human free choices must be choices to *live love* here and now.

    Do I grasp this as the ruling principle of ALL my choices and actions?

V. So, we must have TOTAL INTERIOR FREEDOM
from desires *not* moving us to live love.
Am I this free?
Where do I feel unfree?
Which of my desires feel stronger than my desire to
live love?

VI. Thus, our attitude toward all creatures must be the desire to choose them or to let them go as we must in
order to live love.
Do I have this desire?
Do I at least *desire* to have this desire?
What could I *not* let go of, if I clearly must let it go in
order to live love?

VII. The ROOT desire that *rules* all our choices must be
simply to live love—the perfect love of God and of
other people and of all creatures here and now.
Among all the multidimensional mess of conflicting desires within me, do I experience this as my *root* desire?

2. The retreatant then entered the First Week. For this person,
who spent some forty minutes in the morning and about half
an hour in the evening as daily prayer periods, the first point
of the First Exercise [50] occupied several days, as did the
second [51] and the third points [52] successively. Spiritual
movements during the Second Exercise [55-61] were so powerful and peaceful that the retreatant spent nearly three weeks
doing it. The Third [62-63] and Fourth [64] Exercises continued for two weeks, while the Fifth Exercise [65-72] lasted
another ten days. The grace of the First Week having been
received clearly, it was deepened through praying over appropriate Scripture texts for another week. During the weeks devoted to the First Week of the Exercises, the examination of
conscience [24-43] was explained, the Additional Directions

[73-90] were given, and the Rules for the Discernment of Spirits for the First Week [313-327] were presented.

3. A week was then devoted to the meditation on the Kingdom of Christ [91-100]. Happily, this was just at the beginning of Advent, so the retreatant was able to spend this time in congruence with the liturgy, doing in a slow rhythm of contemplations and repetitions the Incarnation [101-109] and the Visitation [263] and the Advent texts until Christmas. Keeping up this slow rhythm, contemplations of the Infancy narratives [265-270], the Hidden Life [271-272], and the Public Life [273-288] continued until mid-Lent. At the appropriate times the meditations on the Two Standards [136-148] and the Three Classes of Persons [149-157], and the consideration of the Three Kinds of Humility [165-168] were introduced. The Rules for the Discernment of Spirits of the Second Week [328-336] with the complementary Rules for Thinking with the Church [352-370] were explained. For this retreatant the Directions for the Amendment and Reformation of One's Way of Living in One's State of Life [189] was presented.

4. The Third Week occupied the last half of Lent, and the Fourth Week began with the Easter Vigil, continuing through a few successive weeks. The entire Spiritual Exercises were completed by this retreatant in ten months.

Appendix Five

Notes on Directing an Eight-Day Retreat

AN EIGHT-DAY RETREAT USUALLY HAS THE GOAL OF PERSONAL renewal and deepening commitment to one's specific Christian vocation. At times it may involve facing a personal crisis or a particular spiritual need. Such a retreat may enter into the movement of the one Christian spirituality by way of any of the different schools of spirituality. It is an Ignatian retreat if it enters into that movement according to the dynamics and methods and goals of the *Spiritual Exercises.*

When one is directing an eight-day retreat according to the dynamics of the Spiritual Exercises, indeed he or she is "giving the Exercises,"—not the entire month-long Exercises, to be sure—but, nevertheless, using whichever dynamics, methods, and goals within the total movement of the Exercises that fit the stage at which the individual retreatant is *now*. (Cf. [4], [8-11], [18]). Thus, if a person at present simply needs eight days of guided prayer to deepen trust in God, I experience myself as director as "giving the Exercises" to this retreatant by using Ignatian dynamics and methods of prayer to pursue that goal within the total movement of the Spiritual Exercises. If a person at present has need of the particular graces of any of the four weeks of the Exercises, I spend the eight days helping the retreatant to move through the dynamics of that week.

As always, the preliminary conversation with each retreatant is vital, so that the director can know where this retreatant is within the total movement of the Spiritual Exercises and can plan the procedure of this retreat accordingly.

Therefore the director, through experience, must be thoroughly familiar with the dynamics of the total movement of the Spiritual Exercises and thereby prepared to suggest Scripture texts and to present key meditations of the Exercises according to the needs of each retreatant.

For example, if during the preliminary conversation it became clear that the grace of the First Week is already operative in the person, but that deepening of the grace of the Second Week is needed, I begin with a day of bringing the graces of the Principle and Foundation [23] and of the First Week to intense awareness; then I move the retreatant into contemplation of the mysteries of the life of Jesus, focused thematically according to the attitudes of Jesus that this retreatant most needs to grow in at present. Whether or not I include during the last day or two some contemplations from the Third and/or Fourth Weeks of the Exercises depends on the particular needs of this retreatant right now. Giving or not giving any of the key meditations is determined by the same norm.

If what a person needs now is confirmation in living out one's commitment, I take the first day or two to help the retreatant to bring the graces of the Principle and Foundation and of the First and Second Week to intense awareness, according to this person's need. I spend the remainder of the retreat on contemplations from the Third and Fourth Weeks.

However, should the person's needs require it, I spend the entire eight days on the Principle and Foundation and the First Week, or even on the Principle and Foundation alone. At the other extreme, according to a person's needs, I might spend the entire eight days on the Contemplation to Attain Love of God [230-237].

For an annual retreat of renewal of a person with no particular needs discernible at present, other than deepening commitment and intensifying awareness of the movements of the Holy Spirit, I would probably direct the retreatant through a miniversion of the entire Spiritual Exercises, spending more or less time on the mysteries of each week and giving or not giving key meditations, according to the movements experienced within each person.

If the person is in a crisis requiring an election, I would try to place the retreat at the appropriate time, after making sure through ongoing spiritual direction that the person had received the graces necessary before making an election. The retreat itself would consist of making the election, contemplating appropriate mysteries of the life of Jesus, and doing the key meditations of the Second Week, followed during the retreat or after it by contemplation of the mysteries of the Third and Fourth Weeks for the Grace of confirmation. However, I would urge such a person, if at all possible, to make the monthlong Spiritual Exercises, or at least the Exercises according to the Nineteenth Introductory Observation, the "retreat in daily life."

While being prepared for great flexibility in adapting the eight-day retreat to each individual, a director can be helped by having a variety of game plans for eight-day retreats, with appropriate Scripture texts. The following is an example of such a game plan for retreatants who are apostolic religious or priests. This plan is highly flexible and should be adapted freely to the insights and movements given by the Holy Spirit to each individual. *Adaptation is the name of the game.* Thus, the texts and the process indicated here are intended merely as an example, not as the way to direct such a retreat.

An Eight-Day Directed Retreat Plan

Preliminary Conversation[2]

Opening Prayer:
Loving God,
 during this retreat help me to experience
 more than ever before
  what was there from the beginning,
  to hear it,
  to see it with my own eyes,
  to look upon it
   and feel it with my own hands—
 so that I can tell of it powerfully
  to all the persons to whom you send me:
 to make my theme in all my life and words and
  actions the WORD OF LIFE.

Make this life visible to me,
 so that I may see it
  and give my own testimony of it,
  declaring the eternal life which dwelt
  with you, my God,
   made visible to me;
 so that I may share with others
  the life we share with you
  and your Son, Jesus Christ.
       (cf., 1 John 1:1-4)

First Day: The Pattern of God's Fidelity in My Life

 Grace to be prayed for: a deep experience of God's love for you, God's covenant with you, God's unending fidelity to you.

---

2. See Appendix 4.

Advice: If you need it, take a good rest today. In any case make this a relaxing day of entering into the retreat, calming yourself down, allowing the Holy Spirit gently to open you to the graces reserved for you during this retreat.

Take leisurely walks and enjoy the beauty of creation, allowing your senses to open up to awareness of all the variety of this beauty. Notice how created things praise God simply by being what they are, what God has made them to be. Ask God to open you up to be fully yourself, as God has made you.

Prayer: Make Ps. 139 the background for your prayer all day. Ask God, who knows you through and through, to bring to your memory the wonderful things God has done for you throughout your lifetime, your own special sacred history. Try to recognize the pattern of God's fidelity to you personally.[3]

Other Scripture texts for prayer or spiritual direction: Isa. 55:1-3 "Come to the water . . ."; John 14:1-4 Trust in God always; Eph. chaps. 1-3 Universal call to holiness.

Second Day: God's Promise Is a Call to Us to Fidelity in Our Response

Grace to be prayed for: a deep experience of God's personal call to *you* to respond to divine fidelity with absolute fidelity on your part.

Prayer:

1. Gen. 12:1-3—The call of Abraham. God calls you to be ready to leave every known security in order to place all your security only in divine fidelity. Then God will make you a blessing to many people.

2. 1 Sam. 3:1-10—The call of Samuel. "Here I am." "Speak, Lord, your servant hears." Simplicity of totally open response.

---

3. See the presentation of "dynamic memory" in Appendix 1.

3. Luke 1:26-38—The call of Mary. Relying on your Word, let it be as you will.

4. Matt. 5:43-48—"Be perfect as your heavenly Father is perfect . . ."

Other Scripture texts for prayer or spiritual reading: (1) Jesus, model of perfect response: The Servant Songs—Isa. 43:1-4 49:1-6; 50:4-9; 52:1353:12; Luke 4:16-21—"The spirit of the Lord is upon me."; John 17:17-21—"As you have sent me into the world, I have sent them into the world."; Heb. 5:1-10—"He learned obedience in the school of suffering." (2) Heb. chap. 11 Faith of our fathers. (3) Matt. 13:1-23 Parable of the sower.

√ Third Day: Pattern of Your Failure to Respond

Grace to be prayed for: a profound, peaceful, personal sorrow for all your infidelity in responding to God's calls to you, and a deep experience of reconciliation with God, given to you by an unending love shown on the Cross, and, so, the grace to be faithful in the future.

Prayer: Make the background for your prayer all day the scene at the well when Jesus converses with the Samaritan woman, John 4:7-26, 39-42.

Do an exercise of remembering your salvation history, the sins from which Jesus has saved you. Rather than searching in memory to surface these sins yourself, approach Jesus as the woman at the well did.

Let Jesus tell you "everything you ever did"—gently, lovingly, but with total clarity: "You are right," said Jesus, "in saying that you have no husband . . ." (verse 17). As the Holy Spirit brings to mind the events in your history of sinfulness that will be helpful to you now, ask for clarity about the pattern of infidelity and the roots of sin in your life [62-63].

Close each prayer period with Ignatius' colloquy of the first exercise of the First Week [53].

219 / Notes on Directing an Eight-Day Retreat

Other Scripture texts for prayer or spiritual reading: (1) Change of heart: 1 John 1:6-10—"If you claim to be sinless, you are liars . . . he may be trusted to forgive."; Jer. 7:1-8—"Mend your ways that I may live in this place . . . this is the temple of the Lord."; Ezek. 11:17-20—"I will change your heart of stone into a heart of flesh."; Jer. 31:31-34—"I will make a new covenant and write it on your heart." (RECONCILIATION!); Pss. 25, 38, 39, 51. (2) A great Scriptural metaphor: Ezek. chap. 16. (3) Mercy: Phil. 2:5-11—"He made himself nothing, a slave, obedient unto death on a cross."; Isa. 63:7-19—He himself ransomed them; Hos. 11:1-11—"I am God, not man . . ."; Ps. 62— He is my rock of deliverance; Luke 15:1-30—The Prodigal Son. The *only* thing Our Father says to us when we say, "I am sorry," is "Forget it. Let's have a party."

Fourth Day: Peace and Reconciliation

Grace to be prayed for: an even greater deepening of the experience of reconciliation with God and of his peace within you, so that you can share his reconciliation and peace with others.

Prayer: Make the background for your prayer all day: Col. 3:12-17—"You must forgive as the Lord forgave you. Let his peace be judge in your hearts."

For prayer periods, if needed: Matt.9:9-13—Call of Matthew. "I did not come to invite virtuous people, but sinners."; John 8:3-11—Woman taken in adultery. "Nor do I condemn you."; Ezek. 37:1-14—Dry Bones. "I will put my spirit into you and you shall live."; Ps. 16—"You will show me the path to live; in your presence is the fullness of joy."

Other Scripture texts for prayer or spiritual reading: Mark 1:40-45—Cure of the leper. "Of course, I want to!"; Mark 10:46-52—Bartimaeus. "What do you want me to do for you?"; Luke 7:36-50—Mary Magdalen; Luke 19:1-10—Zachaeus. "I

have come to seek the lost."; John 10:1-18—The Good Shepherd
. . . the lost sheep.

Fifth Day: Formation of the Apostles: A Progressive Growth Process of Discovery of the Mystery of the Cross

Grace to be prayed for: Deep interior knowledge of Jesus and passionate personal love of him, in order to respond totally to his call to you to labor with him to bring the Kingdom to be—ready to go with him his way of poverty, humiliations, and humility all the way to the cross.

Prayer:

1. The Vocation of the Apostles [275]—Following the indications given by Ignatius, contemplate the gentle, very patient, but quite inexorable way that Jesus gradually reveals to the apostles the exigencies of the vocation to labor with him. Reflect upon the way that he has been revealing these exigencies to you since you first said "Yes" to his call to follow him. Question Jesus, and wait for him to complete his answer to you:

   > Where do you live? . . . Come and see. Stay . . .
   > Who are you? . . . Word, Way, Truth, Life, Light, King, Shepherd . . .
   > What do you want to do? . . . To struggle under my standard to bring the Kingdom to be for the glory of my Father . . .
   > How do you want to do it? . . . Through poverty, humiliations, humility, the Cross . . .
   > What do you want of me? . . . your heart, yourself . . .

2. Matt. 16:13-28—"Who do people say that the Son of Man is? And you, who do you say I am?" Peter: ". . . the Son of the living God."

After contemplating this mystery, then, imagine Jesus looking into your eyes and asking, "And *you*, what do you say that I am?"

Reflecting not upon book knowledge, but upon all your past experience of Jesus in your own life, answer that question. Many people find it helpful to write down the answer

Other Scripture texts for prayer or spiritual reading: Formation of the Apostles—Appendix 3.

Sixth Day: Ideal of the Apostolic Life

Grace to be prayed for: light on your own concrete living out of your own apostolic call concretely here and now and commitment for the future to live response to this call fully and truly; so that Jesus can work through you and bring the Kingdom to be.

Advice: Hopefully today, with the help of the Holy Spirit, the insights and movements of the retreat days up to now will come together in some form of retreat election.

Prayer: Prayerfully read through Luke, chapters 9 and 10, which show the way of Jesus forming his men into apostles. Select whatever scenes that attract you for your periods of prayer.

Should you need additional material for prayer, take Acts 3:1-16 and contemplate the model given by Peter and John of carrying on the mission of the Lord, who has ascended to his Father until he comes again.

Seventh Day: The Passion

Grace to be prayed for: Compassion with the suffering Jesus: "sorry with Christ in sorrow, anguish with Christ in anguish, tears and deep grief because of the great affliction Christ endures for me," in order that you may be transformed into an active participant in the saving work of Christ continuing today in the Church (cf. [203]).

Prayer: In the way that is most meaningful for you, spend the entire day being with Jesus in his passion and death. You may find it best to choose contemplations for your prayer periods from those suggested by Ignatius [289-2981, or reading through the passion narratives in the four Gospels and selecting scenes for contemplation, or following the Stations of the Cross or the sorrowful mysteries of the rosary.

Throughout the day, ask Jesus to confirm in you the call that you have experienced through the insights and movements of this retreat, through the grace of being with him in his passion and striving "with great effort . . . to grieve, be sad, and weep" [195]

Other Scripture texts for prayer or spiritual reading: See Appendix 3.

Eighth Day: The Risen Lord

Grace to be prayed for: "to be glad and rejoice intensely because of the great joy and the glory of Christ our Lord" [221], and so to be confirmed in the fidelity of your response to his call to you to labor with him in bringing the Kingdom to be in the special way that he calls you at this time.

Advice: Contemplating the Risen Jesus should deepen our love of the Church—the actual human Church through which he continues his mission from the Father until he comes again. It should also deepen in us an authentic apostolic spirit that will shape our lives and words and actions so that, through us, the people to whom we are sent will experience the presence in them of the Spirit of the Risen Jesus.

Prayer: Following the apparitions suggested by Ignatius [299-312], or the accounts of the Risen Jesus in the four Gospels, select scenes for contemplation for your prayer periods.

During the day, in an informal way, go through the contemplation to Attain Love of God [230-237].

Appendix Six

An Eight-Day Communitarian Retreat

THE EIGHT-DAY RETREAT OUTLINED IN THE FOLLOWING PAGES was designed in response to a request from a group of twenty-one Jesuits to give them the Spiritual Exercises, but with the specific goal of enabling them to experience their communitarian spirituality. It was necessary, therefore, to try to provide input and exercises that would enable these Jesuits to move together through the dynamics of the Spiritual Exercises and to discern commonly experienced movements of "various spirits" in order to discover whatever corporate election God might be calling them to make together at this time.

The experience of this retreat was a very positive one for all concerned, including myself as director. It opened up for me a dimension of the Spiritual Exercises that I had never before experienced, at least in the form of a retreat. During recent years I have directed retreats only in the form of the "directed retreat," and I have been deeply impressed by the power of this form of retreat for individual spiritual growth, often with notable communitarian overtones. At the same time, I have experienced the power of corporate spiritual growth generated by workshops in communal spiritual renewal. But this was the first time that I had the opportunity to explore the possibilities of the Spiritual Exercises made corporately. I now feel that such a retreat would be an excellent follow-up for a community after the members of the community have made directed retreats.

What I describe in the following pages is the retreat I actually directed. It was necessary to experiment and design the exercises as the retreat progressed. Others undoubtedly can refine upon, improve, or radically revise these exercises to even more successful effect. Here, however, I felt it most useful simply to narrate how this retreat was actually given.

First, I shall describe the ongoing exercises of this retreat in some detail; then, I shall give the schedule that was followed each day of the retreat.

The Exercises of the Retreat

We began the retreat the evening before the first day with a fifteen minute overview of the retreat. This was intended to explain the goal and design of this retreat as communitarian Spiritual Exercises, to bring the retreatants' expectations or anxieties in accord with the reality of the retreat, and to provide some initial motivation for faith-sharing in small groups. Before the retreat the local man in charge of arrangements had assigned the men to three small groups of seven men each, deliberately mixed as heterogeneously as possible with respect to age, attitudes, backgrounds, and the like. A group leader had been named for each group, and these men met regularly with the director during the retreat to discuss progress or problems and to prepare for the following exercise. The evening continued with a concelebrated Eucharist and concluded with socializing. It was explained to the retreatants that because of the communitarian goals of this retreat talking to one another was an important function of the retreat, just as silence is during a directed retreat.

First Day

The first presentation was ON SPIRITUAL DISCERN-MENT. The focus here was upon the Spiritual Exercises as a spiritual process intended by St. Ignatius to lead the exercitant to a life of finding God in all things—an ongoing life of spiritual discernment, focused when required in an election. This dynamic was briefly applied to the growth of a community as a discerning community, but the thrust of the talk was upon the necessity that each member of a community be truly individually discerning, if this is ever to be possible for the whole community. In reality, this was a presentation of the "Principle and Foundation," with emphasis on the need of Ignatian indifference as the basis of all discernment.

This presentation was immediately followed by forty-five minutes of private prayer in silence. Each man was asked to reflect upon where he NOW found himself in his relation to God and to try to identify one or two texts from the Bible that spoke most meaningfully to him NOW; that is to say, some text that at this time in his life he found powerfully communicating the Word of God to him—a word of comfort or of challenge or of confirmation, etc., depending upon where he NOW found himself before God. Each man was asked to pray over this text and to try to clarify what it was saying to him and why.

Immediately after the prayer period the small groups came together. The group leaders had been prepared to facilitate the sharing and to help men who might initially find faith-sharing difficult. Our experience has consistently been that theoretical objections to faith-sharing or anxieties about it gradually disappear simply through experiencing it. Each man in the group was invited briefly to indicate the text or texts he had prayed over and to express what spoke to him and why. The texts were *indicated,* not read, unless they were very short—simply because of the limits of time. What was shared was not exegesis or interpretation, but *experience.* Therefore, no discussion or challenge on the level of interpretation was permitted, since each man is the only living authority on his own experience. No responses were given to what individual men shared until each man had the opportunity to speak the results of his own prayer. After each one had shared, then, the invitation was given for general sharing; responses to what had been heard, reflections upon the experience of sharing, etc.; finally, if the group felt so moved, the sharing period ended with shared prayer.

The sharing period begins with a moment or two of silence and a prayer for experiencing the presence of the Lord in order to establish a prayerful atmosphere for the sharing. Since this initial sharing period generates the dynamics of this particular group as a faith-sharing group, it is very important that the groups remain the same throughout the retreat, so that each successive experience builds out of and upon the previous experiences of sharing. It is also well before this first meeting to clarify the distinction between faith-sharing and shared prayer. "Shared prayer" means praying to God—addressing God—but sharing my prayer with others by speaking it aloud. "Faith-sharing" means speaking to the group—addressing my brothers and sisters—but speaking about my experience of God.

We went from the period of sharing in small groups to the concelebrated Eucharist. The Eucharist is the heart of each day of the retreat and should be very well prepared. Those who made this retreat remarked that they found the placement of the Eucharist at midday very helpful.

In the afternoon after lunch a couple of hours were provided for individual rest, reflection, sharing, etc. After this, the afternoon presentation was given on THE REALITY OF GOD. This was actually a continuation of the "Principle and Foundation"—that God is All, that God loves us—me!, and some remarks on personal faith-experience of encounter with God. For private prayer, each man was asked to reflect upon and to try to describe to himself: HOW DO I EXPERIENCE MY CHRISTIAN FAITH IN GOD? That is, what are the characteristics or qualities of this experience? How does it feel? What is it like?

During the sharing in small groups, each man tried to express to his brothers his response to this question. This sharing continued until time for the evening meal.

After the evening meal, time was devoted to general sharing in the entire group. During this time there is no reporting of the content of what was shared in the small groups, but everyone is invited to share with all HOW HE FOUND THE EXPERIENCE of this faith-sharing or any insights that he would like to share with all. For this exercise, it is best to put all in a circle, or if the number is large, at least facing one another. The director simply initiates the sharing and thereafter is not active, since it is not a question period but a general sharing period. The evening closed with shared prayer focused on the themes of the day with texts of Scripture such as Sirach 42: 15-24, 43:27-37; Deuteronomy 7:8 ff.; 1 Chronicles 29:10-29; Matthew 5:43-48, 6:26-34. After the shared prayer, there was socializing.

Second Day

The first presentation was on ASCETICISM AND PRAYER TODAY. The thrust was that of the First Week of the Spiritual Exercises, stressing especially the conditions for authentic prayer. During the period of private prayer, each man was asked to reflect very concretely about his prayer at this time of his life: HOW DO I PRAY? It was suggested that he consider *when* he prays, his bodily position for prayer, his *method* of praying, and the like. Finally he was asked out of this prayerful reflection to try to locate the *medium* through which at this time of his life he found God coming to encounter him in his prayer most experientially. Even the greatest mystic encounters God through some medium (even if it be only the medium of dark emptiness) until one sees him face to face after death. So, each one is asked to try to identify the idea of God, or the image of God, or the symbol or the gesture, or Mary or one of the saints, which is most effectively operative as the medium of encounter with God in his prayer NOW—and also to reflect upon how he came to this. During the sharing in the small groups, this is what is shared: the medium of prayer and how I came to it.

The afternoon presentation was on THE DYNAMICS OF INDIVIDUAL SPIRITUAL DISCERNMENT. This continued the dynamics of the First Week of the Spiritual Exercises, stressing openness to the Lord, spiritual freedom, and total surrender in the light of the fact that God loves me just as I am. The process of individual spiritual discernment was also explained. During the private prayer period, each man was invited to look very concretely into his own present life of response to God in order to examine the quality of his indifference and to identify the inordinate affections operative in his life right now. Instead of the sharing in small groups, a communal Penance Service, including sacramental confession and absolution, followed this prayer period. The following was the structure of this service:

Penance Service

1. Hymn

2. Call to Conversion—Ephes. 4:22-24 SILENT REFLECTION

3. Brief Homily SILENT REFLECTION AND PREPARATION FOR INDIVIDUAL REFLECTION

4. Individual Confession and Absolution

5. Communal penance: Prayerful listening to the following readings:

> (a) Ezek. 11:17-20 SILENT REFLECTION
> (b) Ezek. 37:1-14 SILENT REFLECTION

6. Hymn

7. *Close*: "With deep gratitude to the Father for his forgiving love, embodied in Jesus on the Cross, sacramentally reach-

ing us through his Church, let us listen to this word of Paul to us as Church:" Phil. 2:1-11

8. Greeting of Peace

9. Hymn

After the evening meal a presentation was given on SOME TECHNIQUES TO BRING FAITH-EXPERIENCE TO AWARENESS. At the end of this presentation, the focus was given for morning personal prayer and sharing in small groups: the exercise in *dynamic memory*.[4]

After this presentation, the day closed with socializing.

Third Day

Ample time was given in the morning for each retreatant to spend at least one solid hour (preferably more!) doing the exercises in dynamic memory. After this, the small groups came together to spend at least one hour and a half sharing. Each one simply shared with his brothers his present expression of his ongoing faith experience and tried to clarify the meaning of this expression by sharing with them one or two of the key events that enabled him to arrive at this expression through reflection on his own experiences. This was a very rich and joyful sharing, moving the members of the group to great thanksgiving to God who works so wonderfully and so uniquely in each person. This sharing was followed by the celebration of the Eucharist.

The afternoon presentation was on FINDING GOD IN ALL THINGS. This seemed to me the psychological moment in this retreat to focus on the "Contemplation for Obtaining Love": used here not as a "climax" to the entire Exercises, but as a method like the methods of prayer in the appendices of the Exercises to be used as is helpful. The retreatants were invited to review the "contemplation" in their own prayer, and then to

---

4. See Appendix 1.

focus on the question: WHERE DO I NOW FIND GOD MOST EASILY IN CREATURES? The sharing in small groups was the answer of each one to this question. After the evening meal, there was a general sharing ending with shared prayers on Psalm 104, then socializing.

Fourth Day

The morning presentation was titled: ON CHRISTIAN LIFE AND RELIGIOUS LIFE. Its focus was the "Kingdom of Christ" meditation from the Spiritual Exercises. The matter for personal prayer was: WHAT DOES THE CALL OF JESUS CHRIST MEAN TO ME TODAY? HOW DO I SEE MY RELIGIOUS LIFE AS RESPONSE TO HIM? The Eucharist followed the small group sharing

The afternoon presentation was ATTITUDE FOR SPIRITUAL DISCERNMENT. This is a synopsis of the Second Week of the Spiritual Exercises, the contemplation of Jesus in the Gospels, the Two Standards, the Three Classes of Persons, and the Three Kinds of Humility. During the two hours after this presentation, the retreatants were asked to pray privately and to reflect upon the "movements" each had been experiencing during the retreat in order to see whether there was some concrete choice for individual discernment being placed before him by the Lord now. If not, they were invited to review the past year and to try to identify calls to more authentic responses to Jesus Christ as Jesuits and to pray for the gifted strength to respond fully to these calls. This prayer period, then, is analogous to the "Election" time during a private retreat. No small group sharing was scheduled this afternoon.

After the evening meal, there was general sharing followed by shared prayer initiated by reading 1 John 1:1-4.

Fifth Day

On this day the dynamics of the exercises of the retreat were focused in an explicitly corporate way. The morning presentation was on THE DYNAMICS OF COMMUNAL SPIRITUAL DISCERNMENT, stressing the community prerequisites that must be fulfilled before such community spiritual discernment is possible. During the private prayer period, each man was asked to reflect upon his own local community and to try to identify WHERE WE ARE with respect to these prerequisites, and WHAT CONCRETELY CAN WE DO TO BEGIN MOVING TOWARD FULFILLING THEM? Small group sharing followed and, then, the celebration of the Eucharist. Each group listed the results of this sharing on newsprint and posted this for all to see.

The afternoon presentation was on DISCOVERING THE CHARISM OF THE FOUNDER. This develops the four steps involved in coming to a shared experience and communal verbal articulation of the ongoing charism of the religious institute, originated by the Holy Spirit in the founder, continued through the generations in all those called to this common vocation, and existing here and now in the actual members. These four steps are: (1) historical research of the founder; (2) historical research of the community heritage--community dynamic memory; (3) reflection on the expression of the charism in one's brothers or sisters; (4) reflection on the expression of the charism in one's own life. The first two steps will be covered in the following presentation; the third and fourth steps are the matter of prayer and sharing.

The exercise presented for private prayer has three steps:

1. In the presence of God and asking light from the Holy Spirit, I ask myself; WHEN HAVE I FELT MOST AUTHENTICALLY A JESUIT? That is to say, in what event(s), whether in community life or in apostolic service, have I felt that I was *really* being/doing what I am called to? Perhaps at the time I did not reflect upon this, but now,

as I do reflect, what was the event? Ponder it, "taste it," dwell upon it. Now, I ask myself: *WHAT* WAS I BEING/DOING? Not the specific action (which may have been teaching, preaching, or having a party!), but the profound religious identity and mission that I was expressing in and through this action?

2. Then, I ask myself: WHEN IN A BROTHER JESUIT HAVE I SEEN OUR COMMON CALL MOST AUTHENTICALLY EMBODIED? That is to say, in what event(s) in community life or in apostolic services—or simply in the ongoing pattern of a man's life—have I seen truly clear and compelling witnessing, embodiment in life, of what we are called to be/do? Reflect upon this, ponder it. Now, I ask myself: *WHAT* WAS HE BEING/DOING? Not specifically this action, but the profound response to our common call being expressed in and through it?

3. Then, in the light of the reflection upon these experiences, using *my own words* (i.e., deliberately do not turn to the *Constitutions* or other official documents unless their words have become indeed your own!) Complete the sentence: WE JESUITS ARE CALLED. . .

N.B. This statement should be as concise and fundamental a statement as possible of the *basic* common call to be/do that constitutes our religious identity as Jesuits from Ignatius through over four hundred years and in the future: an expression in words of the charism of our founder still active in us today. Write your final expression to take with you to your small group.

The small group sharing has three stages:

1. On arrival in the group, each man writes on newsprint his own verbal expression of the charism he has arrived at through his personal reflection on his experiences. Each one

then reads to all his own expression; and, in order to clarify what he intends to convey through his words, he shares the experience he has reflected upon, either in his own life or in the life of a brother Jesuit. BOTH MAY BE SHARED IF THERE IS SUFFICIENT TIME, BUT OFTEN THERE IS ONLY TIME TO SHARE ONE OF THEM.

2. When all have finished this initial sharing, on another sheet of newsprint note where there is substantial identity of intention in the statements, even though verbal expressions differ (saying the same thing in different words).

3. Now, work together as a group to try to arrive at one common verbal expression of the charism as derived from the shared experiences and expressions of all the members of the group. Bring this final group expression back to the large group on a new piece of newsprint.

   After the evening meal, all come together in the large group to try to bring the statements of all the small groups together in one common expression and affirmation of the charism.

   During the total group sharing, first of all the group leader of each small group explains how his group arrived at its statement. Then, the director invites the retreatants to try to identify substantial identity of intention in the expressions from the various groups. Through open forum discussion, the effort is made finally to arrive at one expression, which all can recognize and affirm as AN expression of the charism of the founder—their own shared charism. When this has been arrived at, the individual members of the entire group should be invited one by one to affirm with the word "YES" that he recognized this statement as AN expression of the common vocation of all. Finally, socializing.

   The men making this retreat came to this *CHARISM STATEMENT*: COMPANIONS OF JESUS AND OF ONE AN-OTHER, WE JESUITS ARE CALLED IN COMPLETE OPEN-

NESS TO THE SPIRIT TO CONTINUE THE MISSION OF CHRIST THROUGH WHOLEHEARTED SERVICE IN THE CHURCH. (N.B. Through general sharing, the rich implications of this statement were clear to all.)

If it is not possible to finish this procedure during the evening session, it should be continued the next morning. From now on, the exercises of the retreat must be flexible enough to allow adjustment to unpredictable time-spans.

Sixth Day

The morning presentation was on THE SCOPE OF OUR VOCATION, a tracing of the religious experience of St. Ignatius himself and of his gradual articulation of this experience as the vocation of the Society of Jesus.

For personal prayer, the men were asked to pray over and to ask the grace of a deepened sense of concrete vocation to apostolic mission as Jesuits here and now. Through this prayer, each one was asked prayerfully to reflect on the Two Standards and to try to identify the actual challenges of the Standard of Satan confronting them here and now in their community and in their work for the Kingdom. Each man listed these and put them into priority order. Here were identified the forces of evil active in the social structures of the place where these Jesuits were missioned.

On arriving in the small group, each man wrote his first three priorities on newsprint and explained how he came to them. Then, each group through corporate reflection made a group list, indicating the three group top priorities. These were posted for all to see in the large group. The morning ended with the celebration of the Eucharist.

The afternoon presentation was ON IDENTIFYING GOALS. This was focused on identifying corporate movements of the Spirit toward a common election. Beginning from the expression of charism, which all had affirmed, it was pointed out that in concretely living out this religious identity, three dimensions are involved: (1) *the quality of personal response* (personal prayer, examen, asceticism, living of poverty, celibacy, obedience, etc.), which generates areas of *personal discernment;* (2) *the quality of community response to religious living* (community life-style here and now), which generates areas of *communal discernment;* (3) *the quality of corporate apostolic mission* (choice and methods of ministries), which generates areas of *communal discernment.*

GOALS were defined as ways to live out our charism in being/doing, which emerge into common consciousness through corporate reflection upon: (1) our charism as expressed in our common articulation of it; (2) problems and obstacles identified; (3) challenges recognized. To identify these goals, then, requires looking at the actual evidence here and now: *where we are now* as a religious community called to corporate mission, what the "signs of our times" are: the needs of people, others meeting these needs, our own personal and material resources, and so forth. The caution is given when trying to identify goals to think in terms of *desirability* rather than *feasibility* (the latter will clearly emerge during deliberation on specific means, but to consider it here will destroy creative thinking), and also constantly to keep our charism in mind—that is to say, that we are not the whole Church and are not called to do *everything,* but rather to respond to our specific call to share the mission of Jesus.

A *GOAL* refers to a way to live the charism that is UNANIMOUSLY recognized now as a specific call from God to all the members of the group. It is vital that it be clear that each person understands every word in the statement of the goal the same way. A *MEANS,* or "HOW TO," refers to a possible way that is not recognized unanimously by all members as a call here and now. These will be matters for deliberation about means to achieve goals.

Goals should be put into priority order by considering which are: (a) impossible *now*; (b) long term; (c) middle term; (d) short term, and according to their *importance* and their *urgency.* Through ongoing deliberations, what are now "HOW TO's" will come to be recognized and affirmed as GOALS, and what is now impossible or long term will become possible and shorter term. Proposals for deliberation can be generated only after GOALS have been clearly affirmed.

After this presentation, the prayer period was devoted to the following directions:

1. In the presence of God and praying for light from the Holy Spirit, each man reviews personal and communal experiences and movements during this retreat.

2. Each one asks the Holy Spirit to enlighten him concerning any *call* the Spirit may be communicating to this group *as a group,* through the personal and communal movements of which he is aware.

3. In light of the evidence that has emerged (and is posted on newsprint) with respect to (a) Jesuit community life in the local communities at present; (b) Jesuit apostolic ministry here and now, see whether any *specific calls* from God emerge in your own consciousness. If so, pray over these.

4. Write down your expression of these calls under (a) Community and (b) Mission.

5. Put these into priority order and endeavor to indicate the first three priorities as you see them in prayer.

There were four steps in the small group sharing:

1. Each man wrote on newsprint his first three priorities. Each one then explained how he came to these in his prayer and clarifies the meaning of each.

2. The group as a whole then endeavored to identify where there was unanimous awareness of the same calls.

3. The group identified the first three priorities in this common list of experienced calls.

4. Any calls reported by individuals, but not unanimously experienced, we listed separately. These possibly indicated calls that will emerge as common in the future. Final results were posted for the entire group to see.

After the evening meal, the entire group worked with the results of the small groups until a common goal emerged and was affirmed by all as a unanimous experience of a specific call from God. The goal affirmed by this group of Jesuits was: TO IMPROVE THE QUALITY OF THE RELIGIOUS DIMENSION OF OUR LOCAL COMMUNITIES.

The goal signified to this group a unanimous awareness of a call from God to provide mutual support and challenge to one another in corporate living out of the scope of our vocation. All felt that the quality of this support and challenge was actually lacking greatly in relation to the call experienced. Although there was some unanimity about calls to apostolic mission, it was seen that evidence was lacking for generating a clear proposal for deliberation in this area; while the evidence for the community area was clear.

The evening ended with socializing.

Seventh Day

The morning presentation was ON THE METHOD OF DELIBERATION. This stressed necessary attitudes of interior freedom, really listening to one another, and so forth, and explained the deliberation process. Each small group then elected a Task Force member and brainstormed for fifteen minutes on possible means or "HOW TO's" to accomplish the goal all had affirmed. The Task Force then worked for forty-five minutes to generate a proposal for deliberation. The other men were invited to listen to the Task Force or to pray during this time. The proposal for deliberation was then presented to the entire group, making sure that each man understood each word the same way.

Following this, each man spent the time until the celebration of the Eucharist in personal, prayerful discernment of the proposal. After the noon meal, all were invited to continue this personal discernment until 3:00 p.m. At this time, the communal deliberation began and continued until time for the evening meal, after which the results of the deliberation of each small group were posted on newsprint for the entire group to see. The rest of the evening was spent in working through the differences in results. Before this was completed, it was interrupted for socializing and a night of sleep.

Eighth Day

Each man had been asked the night before to pray before the morning session and to try to identify movements he experienced with respect to what he had heard the evening before. Deliberation continued in the entire group throughout most of the morning, with breaks for prayer when these seemed necessary. Although I had prepared exercises for this morning if needed, I dropped them since it is necessary to be very flexible once this stage of the retreat has been reached. One does not hurry the Holy Spirit!

Finally, all the retreatants unanimously affirmed the following corporate election:

ALL OF US IN OUR LOCAL COMMUNITIES, INVITING OTHERS, COMMIT OURSELVES TO COME TOGETHER ONCE A WEEK FOR ABOUT AN HOUR, TO GIVE MUTUAL SUPPORT ON THE SPIRITUAL DIMENSION, THROUGH CONCELEBRATED MASS OR OTHER SPIRITUAL EXERCISES.

All understood that each one was committing himself to be present in the local community gatherings indicated. Other members of these communities not in attendance at this retreat would be invited, but not pressured, to share in these gatherings. At this point, the persons from the same local communities met together to specify their own commitment as to day of the week, hour of the day, possible ways to plan the focus of their gatherings, and so forth. They were also asked to explore possible ways to be accountable to the entire group of men who had made this retreat and this election together.

The retreatants affirmed as the method of mutual accountability: (a) Every two months to send a written report of their local community gatherings to one man, who would compile and multiply these reports and send them to the various groups; (b) During the Christmas vacation, and again during the Easter vacation, to come together for one full day to share their experiences with one another.

We then went to the noon meal.

The presentation in the afternoon was called GROWTH IN APOSTOLIC HOLINESS, an overview of the working of the Holy Spirit in the life of a person called to apostolic community from the beginning until death, stressing the special kinds of "dark nights" belonging to the apostolic vocation. This was followed by shared prayer.

Then there was half an hour of general sharing about the experiences of the retreat. Perhaps the most moving remarks were those of the oldest retreatant, that: "this indeed was truly the Spiritual Exercises," and what a strengthening and consoling experience it was to make a "retreat resolution" with the entire group and to be able to rely upon one another for being called to fidelity and supported mutually in it.

The retreat closed with a beautiful concelebration of the Eucharist offering thanks and asking confirmation from God of the corporate election.

The Design of the Retreat in Detail

Preliminary Evening

7:30-7:45	BRIEF OVERVIEW OF THE RETREAT
8:00	Eucharist, followed by socializing

First Day

9:00-9:45	ON SPIRITUAL DISCERNMENT
9:45-10:30	Private Prayer
10:30-11:30	Share in small groups
11:45	Eucharist
12:30	Meal
3:00	Coffee
3:30-4:15	THE REALITY OF GOD
4:15-5:15	Private Prayer
5:15-6:16	Share in small groups
6:30	Meal
7:30	Share in entire group, followed by shared prayer. Socializing.

Second Day

9:00-9:45	ON ASCETICISM AND PRAYER TODAY
9:45-10:30	Private Prayer
10:30-11:30	Share in small groups
11:45	Eucharist
12:30	Meal
3:00	Coffee

3:30-4:30	THE DYNAMICS OF INDIVIDUAL SPIRITUAL DISCERNMENT
4:30-5:30	Private Prayer
5:45	Penance Service
6:30	Meal
7:30	SOME TECHNIQUES TO BRING FAITH EXPERIENCE TO AWARENESS

Third Day

Before 9:45	At least one solid hour of private prayer
9:45-11:30	Share in small groups
11:45	Eucharist
12:30	Meal
3:00	Coffee
3:30-4:15	Private Prayer
5:15-6:15	Share in small groups
6:30	Meal
7:30	Share in entire group, followed by shared prayer. Socializing

Fourth Day

9:00-9:45	ON CHRISTIAN LIFE AND RELIGIOUS LIFE
9:45-10:30	Private Prayer
10:30-11:30	Share in small groups
11:45	Eucharist
12:30	Meal
3:00	Coffee
3:30-4:30	ATTITUDES FOR SPIRITUAL DISCERNMENT
4:30-6:15	Private prayer and reflection

6:30	Meal
7:30	Share in entire group, followed by shared prayer. Socializing.

Fifth Day

9:00-9:45	THE DYNAMICS OF COMMUNAL SPIRITUAL DISCERNMENT
9:45-10:30	Private Prayer
10:30-11:30	Share in small groups
11:45	Eucharist
12:30	Meal
2:30	Coffee
3:00-4:00	DISCOVERING THE CHARISM OF THE FOUNDER
4:00-5:00	Private Prayer
5:00-6:15	Share in small groups
6:30	Meal
7:30	Put together results. Socializing.

Sixth Day

9:00-9:45	THE SCOPE OF OUR VOCATION
9:45-10:30	Private Prayer
10:30-11:30	Share in small groups
11:45	Eucharist
12:30	Meal
3:00	Coffee
3:30-4:00	ON IDENTIFYING GOALS
4:00-5:00	Private Prayer
5:00-6:15	Share in small groups
6:30	Meal

7:30 Put together results. Select a goal for deliberation. Socializing.

Seventh Day

9:00-9:45 ON THE METHOD OF DELIBERATION

9:30-9:45 Select Task Force and Brainstorm in Small Groups

9:45-10:30 Task Force generates proposal for Deliberation

10:30-11:00 Present proposal for Deliberation

11:00-11:45 Personal discernment of proposal

11:45 Eucharist

12:30 Meal
CONTINUE PRIVATE DISCERNMENT

2:30 Coffee

3:00-6:15 Do deliberation in small groups

6:30 Meal

7:30 Work on putting together results in large groups. Socializing.

Eighth Day

9:00-12:15 Bring corporate election to terminus; specify details for local communities; agree upon method of mutual accountability. (SEE BELOW**)

12:30 Meal

3:00 Coffee

3:30-4:45 GROWTH IN APOSTOLIC HOLINESS followed by shared prayer

4:45-5:15 Share in entire group

5:30 Closing Eucharist

**Exercises prepared for the eighth morning, but dropped because of the need for flexibility to complete the corporate elections:

9:00-9:45   JESUIT PERSON AND JESUIT COMMUNITY

9:45-10:30   Private Prayer (*Focus*: What does Jesuit obedience mean to me?) 10:30-11:30 Share in small groups 11:45-12:15 JESUIT OBEDIENCE

Some Reference Materials

N.B. I am deeply convinced both in giving retreats and in giving renewal workshops that effectiveness depends upon each director speaking from one's own experience in one's own words. Nevertheless, it may be useful here to indicate places where materials that were the base of my own presentations during this retreat can be found. These are some of my own writings .

I. Brief Overview and On Spiritual Discernment

"Ignatian Discernment," *Studies in the Spirituality of Jesuits*, Vol. II, No. 2, pp. 47-88 (The American Assistancy Seminar on Jesuit Spirituality, St. Louis, 1970).

"The Dynamics of Individual Ignatian Discernment," *Dossier "Deliberatio" B* (Centrum Ignatian Spiritualists, Rome, 1972), pp. 193-206.

"The Still, Small Voice," *The Way*, II, No. 4 (October, 1971), pp. 275-282 .

II. Some Techniques to Bring Faith-Experience to Awareness

"Some Techniques to Identify and Clarify Personal, Core Faith-Experience," *Dossier "Deliberatio" B* (CIS, Rome, 1972), pp. 173-182.

III. Finding God in All Things

"Deliberatio Communitaria: 'Finding God in All Things,' " *Dossier "Deliberatio" B* (CIS, Rome, 1972), pp. 184-192.

IV. On Christian Life and Religious Life

"Reflections on Religious Life," *Review for Religious*, Vol. 38, No. 5 (September, 1969), pp. 705-718.

"Ignatian Attitudes for Discernment," *Communal Discernment: New Trends, Subsidia Ad Discernendum*, No. 14 (Rome: Centrum Ignatianum Spiritualitatis, 1975), pp. 35-44.

V. The Dynamics of Communal Spiritual Discernment

"Communal Discernment: Reflections on Experience," *Studies in the Spirituality of Jesuits*, Vol. IV, No. 5 (St. Louis, 1972), pp. 159-192.

VI. Discovering the Charism of the Founder

"Discovering the Founder's Charism," *Supplement to the Way*, No. 14 (Autumn, 1971), pp. 62-70.

VII. The Scope of Our Vocation

Making an Apostolic Community of Love: The Role of The Superior according to St. Ignatius of Loyola (The Institute of Jesuit Sources, St. Louis, 1970), Ch. I, "Service of Christ through Apostolic Love," pp. 13-38.

Ch. II, "Apostolic Love in Companionship," pp. 39-55. Also, "To be Together . . . in Spite of Everything," *Review for Religious*, Vol. 32, No. 3, pp. 514-521.

VIII. On Identifying Goals

"Ignatian Vision: Discernment of the *Magis*," *The Preamble* (JSEA, Washington, D.C., 1971).

"Deliver Us from Evil: The Social Welfare Mission of Religious Communities Today," *Review for Religious*, Vol. 30, No. 5 (September, 1971), pp. 863-875.

IX. On the Method of Deliberation

See number V above.